Gertrude Jekyll and the Country House Garden

JUDITH B. TANKARD

From the archives of Country Life

AURUM PRESS

First published in Great Britain 2011 by Aurum Press Limited
7 Greenland Street, London NW1 0ND
www.aurumpress.co.uk

ISBN 978 1 84513 624 6
10 9 8 7 6 5 4 3 2 1
2015 2014 2013 2012 2011

Originated, printed and bound in Singapore

Previous pages: *Munstead Wood in Surrey, Gertrude Jekyll's home.*

THE COUNTRY LIFE PICTURE LIBRARY

The *Country Life* Picture Library holds a complete set of prints made from its
negatives, and a card index to the subjects, usually recording the name of the
photographer and the date of the photographs catalogued, together with a
separate index of photographers. It also holds a complete set of *Country Life*
and various forms of published indices to the magazine. The Library may be
visited by appointment, and prints of any negatives it holds can be supplied
by post.

For further information, please contact the Library Manager, Justin
Hobson, at *Country Life*, Blue Fin Building, 110 Southwark Street, London
SE1 0SU (*Tel:* 020 3148 4474).

ACKNOWLEDGEMENTS

I would like to thank Kathryn Bradley-Hole for inviting me to write this book
and Clare Howell, my editor at Aurum Press. This book could not have been
written without the assistance of Justin Hobson, library manager of *Country
Life* Picture Library, and his staff who helped me sort through hundreds of
possible illustrations.

There are a number of people who generously shared their knowledge
of Gertrude Jekyll and her circle of friends, welcomed me to their gardens,
or assisted me in other ways. These include Jane Balfour, Gordon Barnes,
Adrian Bird, Mary Caröe, Sir Robert and Lady Clark, Helena Gerrish,
Miranda Hambro, Peter Herbert, Robert Mallet, Sir Nicholas Mander Bt.,
the late J-P Marix-Evans, Gail Naughton, Sebastian Nohl, Nan Blake Sinton,
Rosamund Wallinger, David Wheeler, Philip White, Rosaleen Wilkinson,
and Martin Wood. I owe a great debt to the Lutyens Trust, which over the
past twenty-five years provided me with opportunities to visit all the
Lutyens properties but one discussed in this book. In particular our excursion
to Lambay Castle in 2005 was most memorable for the beauty of the site and
the chance to see Lutyens's inimitable detailing in the various buildings.

My personal library, which includes a near-complete run of *Country Life*
magazine and multiple editions of all the books published by Country Life
(which I wrote about in *Hortus*), greatly facilitated my work. I have also
benefited from the scholarly research and writings of Primrose Arnander,
Richard Bisgrove, Jane Brown, Fenja Gunn, Mervyn Miller, David Ottewill,
Margaret Richardson, Jane Ridley, Michael Tooley, Robin Whalley, Martin
Wood, and numerous other authors.

But most of all I continue to learn from Gertrude Jekyll, whose books and
articles never fail to surprise and delight me, no matter how many times I've
read them.

LIST OF ARTICLES

This is a list of primary articles in *Country Life* for which the photographs
reproduced in this book were specially taken. The photographer's name is
given in brackets, where known.

Barrington Court, Somerset: 24 May 2007 (Will Pryce).
Le Bois des Moutiers, Normandy: 25 March 2009 (Will Pryce).
Bridge House, Surrey: 1 April 1916.
Cleeve Prior Manor, Worcestershire: 26 May and 9 June 1900.
Deanery Garden, Berkshire: 9 May 1903 (Charles Latham).
Easton Lodge, Essex: 23 November 1907; 1 May 1909.
Folly Farm, Berkshire: 28 January and 4 February 1922 (Sleigh).
Gledstone Hall, Yorkshire: 20 April 1935 (A. E. Henson).
Goddards, Surrey: 30 January 1904.
Gravetye Manor, Sussex: 23 March 1918.
Great Tangley Manor, Surrey: 20 July and 6 August 1898 (F. M. Good);
    21 January 1905.
Hestercombe Gardens, Somerset: 17 October 1908; 16 April 1927
    (A. E. Henson); to be published in 2011 (Paul Barker).
Heywood, Abbeyleix, Co. Laois: 4 January 1919.
Hurtwood, Surrey: 18 November 1911.
Iford Manor, Wiltshire: 26 August and 2 September 1922 (Sleigh); 4 April
    1963; 18 May 1972 (Jonathan Gibson).
Lambay Castle, Co. Dublin: 4 May 1912; 20 July 1929 (A. E. Henson).
Lindisfarne Castle, Northumberland: 9 September 2004 (Val Corbett).
The Manor House, Upton Grey, Hampshire: to be published in 2011
    (Paul Barker).
Marsh Court, Hampshire: 19 April 1913; 26 March 1932 (Gill).
Mathern Palace, Monmouthshire: 19 November 1910.
Mount Stewart, Co. Down: 12 October 1935 (Gill).
Mounton House, Monmouthshire: 13 and 20 February 1915.
Munstead Wood, Surrey: 8 December 1900 (Charles Latham); 15 May 1997;
    12 March 1998; to be published in 2011 (Paul Barker, autumn photographs;
    Julian Nieman, spring/summer photographs).
Orchards, Surrey: 11 April 1908 (Charles Latham).
Owlpen Manor, Gloucestershire: 6 October 1906; 2 November 1951
    (A. E. Henson).
Plumpton Place, Sussex: 20 May 1933.
Queen's Dolls' House: 9 February 1924.
St. Catherine's Court, Somerset: 24 December 1898; 24 November and
    1 December 1906 (Charles Latham).
Tigbourne Court, Surrey: 23 September 1905.
Townhill Park, Hampshire: 21 April 1923.
Valewood Farm, Surrey: 21 September 1935 (A. E. Henson and Mason).
Vann, Surrey: 24 June 1912; 27 May 1976 (Alex Starkey); 26 June 1986.
Warley Place, Essex: 8 May 1915 (Reginald A. Malby).
Westbrook, Surrey: 20 January 1912.
Woodhouse Copse, Surrey: 16 October 1926.

The following gardens were first published in Country Life books:
Bishopsbarns, York: *Small Country Houses of Today* (1910); Highmount, Surrey;
Little Boarhunt, Hampshire; and Millmead, Surrey: *Gardens for Small Country
Houses* (1912).

Contents

Introduction

....

"The love of gardening is a seed that once sown never dies."

....

The central portion of Gertrude Jekyll's main flower border at Munstead Wood, Surrey, is ablaze with warm-toned plants, such as dahlias and gladioli.

In 1932, *Country Life*'s architectural writer, H. Avray Tipping, wrote a touching tribute to England's most famous gardener, Gertrude Jekyll: 'Who of us that are gardeners to-day have not profited by the experience and teaching of this entirely capable woman, easily efficient in all she set out to know and to do? She opened our eyes to the possibilities of the herbaceous border, of the woodland garden, of the bulb-set glade'. '… She was no mere theorist, but a practical worker [and] her books are the fruits of long experience, critically treated and plainly set forth.'

Jekyll has been hailed as 'the grand old lady of English gardening' and praised for being a true artist with an exquisite sense of colour. Her inimitable books were singled out as the 'most perfect example of practical wisdom in combination with poetical thought.' But Russell Page cut to the bone when he said, 'I can think of few English gardens made in the last fifty years which do not bear the mark of her teaching.' Jekyll's own garden at Munstead Wood inspired legions of budding designers, from Page to Mein Ruys, while her books were considered essential to every true gardener's library, and that remains so today.

Who was this remarkable woman who allegedly changed the face of England? She was an artist, a gardener, a designer, a writer, and much more. Her appreciation of architecture helped form her ideas about garden design and her exceptionally keen skills of observation enabled her to appreciate the minutiae of the smallest seed, a subtle design defect, or whatever else struck her fancy. Above all, Jekyll was a lover of the English countryside and in particular old West Surrey – its landscape, buildings, and traditions. She extolled nature in her many articles and books and shared this passion with her circle of friends, which included artists, horticulturists, gardeners, musicians, writers, and architects. Her fascination with old manor houses and their simple courtyard enclosures shaped her vision of the inseparability of house and garden, a

Left: Classic Jekyll-style double herbaceous borders at The Manor House at Upton Grey, Hampshire.

Above: Gertrude Jekyll (1843–1932) was the grand old lady of English gardening when her portrait was painted by William Nicholson in 1921.

vision shared by a generation of younger artists and architects associated with the Arts and Crafts movement. In the end she became a champion of what is now referred to as Arts and Crafts gardens, which were intimate in scale and attuned to local materials and traditions.

Jekyll's longtime association with *Country Life* helped spread the word about this new approach to home and garden design, and nowhere was this more evident than in the magazine's promotion of the architectural career of Edwin Lutyens, her primary collaborator in garden design. Her numerous garden articles and books, some of which she wrote in collaboration with *Country Life* architectural editors, Lawrence Weaver and Christopher Hussey, were filled with practical advice and aesthetic guidelines. It is fair to say that without Jekyll, the history of garden design in general and *Country Life* in particular would certainly have been poorer.

*   *   *

Gertrude Jekyll was born in 1843 in London, in the heart of Mayfair. When she was five years old her family moved to Bramley, a small village in West Surrey, and it was here that she developed an enduring passion for outdoor life and for all the old traditions of Surrey, from building methods to cottage gardens. As a youngster, she led a solitary life and was left to her own devices to explore the woods, meadows, and heaths that were ablaze with wildflowers. Her two younger brothers were away at school while she was growing up, and her older sister Caroline moved to Venice, where she and her husband, Frederick Eden, had a famous garden on the Giudecca. Gertrude's father, Captain Edward Jekyll, instilled in his daughter a sense of curiosity and independence, while her mother, Julia Hammersley, gave her daughter a lifelong appreciation of music and the arts.

As a young woman, Jekyll set her heart on becoming a painter and fell under the spell of John Ruskin and J. M. W. Turner. She attended the South Kensington School of Art and before long was exhibiting her paintings. Soon her ever-widening circle of London friends included George Frederick Watts and Frederic Leighton. When she was barely nineteen, she travelled with friends to Greece and Turkey, a journey that opened her eyes to the delights of foreign travel and landscapes. Later on she visited France and Italy where she learned various crafts, including wood inlay and gilding. The artist George Leslie described Jekyll in 1881 as a young woman with many singular and remarkable accomplishments, including carving, carpentry, smith's work, and *repoussé* work. She also excelled at fine embroidery and executed designs for the Royal School of Needlework, as well as for some of her artist friends. This eventually led to trying her hand at textile and wallpaper design, perhaps stimulated by her visit to William Morris's studio in 1869. As if that weren't enough, she designed jewellery, with intricate and delicate motifs derived from Greek and Roman examples she sketched in museums. All this practical experience relating to design, detail, and colour would serve her well when she eventually turned her attention to landscape gardening.

Winters in Algiers with her friend, the artist Barbara Bodichon, found Jekyll in pursuit of local plants. Beginning in 1873 she spent holidays in Switzerland with Jacques and

Top: *Les Maures from St Cassien Near Cannes*, *painted by Gertrude Jekyll on her sketching expedition to the French Riviera in 1868.*

Above: *Gertrude Jekyll's watercolour of Bougainvillea, painted in the 1870s when she visited Algiers.*

Right: *Gertrude Jekyll as a young woman seated on a wheelbarrow outside Higham Bury, Bedfordshire, home of her brother Edward Jekyll.*

Léonie Blumenthal, musical friends from London, who in turn introduced her to the English watercolour artist, Hercules Brabazon Brabazon, who influenced her colour palette. Years later she acknowledged her debt to him, and after she embarked on gardening in earnest, she told him that she was 'doing some rigorous landscape gardening … doing living pictures with land and trees and flowers.'

Little survives of Jekyll's early craftwork, but various scrapbooks and albums reveal her talents as a designer and artist. Watercolours of her Mediterranean travels (kept in the Surrey History Centre in Woking) are especially revealing as they show her impressionistic response to the landscape, as well as her fascination with striking foliage plants, such as agaves, opuntias, asphodels, and aloe. On a trip to the French Riviera she sketched the stands of umbrella pines, the olive-green foliage and reddish-brown bark of the trees shown against the azure-blue mountains in the background. In Algiers, she sketched the countryside, with white houses highlighted against navy blue skies. She began collecting botanical specimens on her rambles in and around Algiers, including the tiny, blue-flowering *Iris scorpioides*. Her nephew, Francis Jekyll, later mused that her 'susceptibility to colour and composition reached its high-water mark' during her excursions to Algiers. All of this proved good preparation for her inimitable garden compositions, but she soon discovered that most of the Mediterranean plants she admired failed to acclimatize in England.

In 1876 Jekyll's mother, by then a widow, decided to build a new house not far from Bramley on Munstead Heath. The architectural style of the house, which was dismissed by Pevsner as 'Parsonage Gothic', could not have been more different from the home that she herself would build twenty years later at Munstead Wood. At Munstead House, as her mother's home was called, Jekyll had a spacious workshop with cabinets filled with exotic woods and other materials, as well as fabric samples for interior design commissions. Books and pottery collected from her travels abroad filled the shelves and the walls were lined with her paintings. For a single woman approaching her fortieth birthday, she could work in peace and quiet on her various projects and entertain her friends from London. After moving in she wrote in her diary – 'to Munstead for good.'

During her years at Munstead House, from 1876 until 1895, when her mother died, Jekyll's gardening interests grew. She assisted with the laying out of the grounds, and the mistakes she made were not repeated at Munstead Wood, where she moved in 1897. As her activities in embroidery and other crafts slowly declined (possibly due to problems with her eyesight), she threw herself into intensive botanical

studies which often brought her into contact with like-minded enthusiasts. Her workshop was soon flooded with specimens sent by other collectors. In 1880 the influential gardening writer and editor, William Robinson, and the rose expert, Reynolds Hole (later Dean of Rochester), visited Munstead House. Two years later Robinson sent his assistant editor, William Goldring, to write an article about the gardens for *The Garden*. 'In the midst of wild heath land, diversified with picturesque clusters of Hollies, Scotch Firs, wild Junipers, and a variety of other spontaneous growth is a beautiful garden made by a lady within the past four years, and along the whole range of the Surrey sandstone hills there could scarcely have been found a better position for a house and garden than this,' he wrote. Goldring extolled the capital use of carefree hardy plants, the ease of access to various parts of the garden, and, above all, the extraordinary hardy flower border: 'Never before have we seen hardy plants set out so well or cultivated in such a systematic way.' It was 'the richest and most effective border of hardy flowers that we know of near London.'

This was high praise for a gardener who seemed to burst upon the scene in the early 1880s. But her new reputation was based on a solid foundation of horticultural knowledge, as

well as design sensibilities that had been percolating for years. Her knowledge came in part from her systematic gardening pursuits and her training as an artist, but some of the practical aspects derived from her friendship with Robinson. They first met in 1875, when she called at his office in Covent Garden where he edited *The Garden*, one of several magazines he founded. Soon afterwards, she began sending in plants for identification, which led to her writing botanical notes for the magazine under the initials 'G J'. In 1881 her by-line had expanded to 'G. Jekyll, Munstead, Godalming' when she wrote a longer piece entitled 'Some Plants from Algeria'. From this modest start, Jekyll was soon propelled to the forefront of garden writing.

William Robinson, who was only five years her senior, was an authority to be reckoned with. He already had several books to his credit when he met Jekyll, notably *The Wild Garden* (1870), which caught her fancy because it praised the beauty of hardy, native plants in their natural settings as opposed to annuals planted in elaborate carpet-like patterns. The book influenced her ideas about garden design in general, as well as the layout of Munstead House, and later Munstead Wood. Gravetye Manor, Robinson's home in Sussex, served

as an example of the ideal relationship of house, lawn, and garden with the surrounding landscape. Although it was on a much larger scale than Munstead Wood – in its heyday the estate extended to 1,000 acres – or any of the gardens that she would eventually design, the lessons were still applicable. Elaborate formal gardens filled to bursting with thousands of favourite plants hugged the large, rambling Elizabethan manor house. These gardens were enclosed with trellises and pergolas smothered with roses and clematis. Where the ground rose behind the manor, Robinson used heathers, ornamental grasses, shrubs, and distinctive trees in an informal landscape setting. Most of the surrounding grounds, however, were open fields filled with spring bulbs and native plants and carefully managed woodlands. For its day, it was an amazing example of how one could gracefully combine both formal and informal elements in a designed landscape. Compared to the vast expanses of bedded-out annuals that

Above: *Sweeps of daffodils at Gravetye Manor, Sussex, home of the noted gardening writer and editor William Robinson (1838–1935), whose book* The Wild Garden *favoured a naturalistic approach to gardening.*

Right: *Drifts of narcissus in Ellen Willmott's rock garden at Warley Place, Essex, at one time one of the most remarkable gardens in England.*

characterized Victorian estate gardens, Gravetye Manor was certainly revolutionary. Jekyll was a frequent visitor in the early days when Robinson was laying out the grounds, and in later years they kept in touch through letters.

Ellen Ann Willmott, with whom Gertrude Jekyll shared the distinction of being among the first gardeners to be honoured with the RHS Victoria Medal of Honour in 1897, was a friend of Robinson's and part of her own circle of friends. Willmott's extensive gardens at Warley Place in Essex, which were paid for by a grand inheritance that was later squandered, were the equal of Gravetyc Manor and Munstead Wood. Together these are the three most important gardens of the era. Willmott's passion for plants and her renown as a botanical authority catapulted her to the top echelon of gardeners. As Jekyll wrote in *Country Life* in 1910, 'Unremitting care and thought, applied with the owner's rare intelligence, consummate knowledge and extraordinary personal energy, have … produced a garden that stands alone in beauty and interest.' This was high praise from Jekyll whose critical eye rarely missed a detail. Willmott's books, *Warley Garden in Spring and Summer* (published in 1909 and illustrated with her own photographs) and *The Genus Rosa* (published in parts between 1910 and 1914), are all that remain of her once-famous garden.

In 1885, Jekyll took up the relatively new art of photography and the first winter found her photographing plants at Munstead House, as well as in neighbouring villages where she admired cottage gardens and the local villagers who tended them. For Jekyll, photography became an extension of her art training and taught her composition and observation skills necessary to identify and appreciate plants. It also provided her with a new vocation for writing articles and books about gardening that were illustrated with her own photographs, rather than using cheap chromolithograph plates, which were on the wane. Robinson's books, which were primarily illustrated with line drawings by hired artists, such as Alfred Parsons, have neither the literary flair nor the visual appeal of Jekyll's. Books by her Surrey neighbour, Marie Theresa Earle, namely *Pot-Pourri From a Surrey Garden* (1898) and its sequels, were charming in their own way, but they never really caught on to the extent that Jekyll's did.

It was clear when Jekyll's first book, *Wood and Garden*, appeared in 1899 that it was in a league of its own. In the introduction to the book she modestly explained that there were already many good books about gardening, but because there was a growing interest in the subject she felt justified in contributing another one. 'I have lived among outdoor flowers for many years,' she wrote, and 'rejoice when I see any one, and especially children, inquiring about flowers, and wanting gardens of their own.' Her book was the product of years of practical experience and her comments were paired with specific photographs that precisely illustrated her points. She would use this same formula for most of her subsequent books, notably *Home and Garden* (1900), *Old West Surrey* (1904), *Children and Gardens* (1908), and her most influential book of all, *Colour in the Flower Garden* (1908), as well as for the larger, more elaborate volumes she wrote in collaboration with *Country Life* writers and editors, such as *Gardens for Small Country Houses* (1912) with Lawrence Weaver and *Garden Ornament* (1927) with Christopher Hussey.

One wonders if Jekyll's fame as a garden writer would have been the same without *Country Life*. She enjoyed a long and enduring relationship with the magazine, beginning around 1899 until a few years before her death in 1932, rivalling Christopher Lloyd's long-running, popular gardening columns in more recent times. In all she wrote more than one hundred signed articles or notes for the magazine and published nine books. She also wrote hundreds of articles for *The Garden* and *Gardening Illustrated*, both one-time affiliates of *Country Life*. She first met Edward Hudson, the magazine's founder and proprietor, in the summer of 1899 when he and his gardens editor, E. T. Cook, paid a visit to Munstead Wood. As a result of the visit, Hudson persuaded Jekyll to contribute 'Garden Notes' to the magazine and also to co-edit *The Garden* with Cook, which she did for a year before giving up due to the pressure of her own work.

Hudson, who had a strong personal interest in gardens and in country matters, had founded the magazine in 1897. He had a finely-tuned artistic sensitivity and an extraordinary instinct for selecting associates. In Gertrude Jekyll he sensed a woman of many accomplishments, from writing and gardening to architecture and design. In 1900 Jekyll introduced Hudson to her young friend, Edwin Lutyens. Hudson, of course, not only commissioned several houses and gardens from Lutyens, but also championed his work in the pages of *Country Life* to the exclusion of almost all other architects. Hudson also recognized the talents of Avray Tipping, who was *Country Life*'s architectural writer for over twenty-five years, from 1907 until his death in 1933, when he was succeeded by Christopher Hussey. Tipping, a prolific author,

came to be a great admirer of Jekyll. 'In a series of books,' he wrote, 'Gertrude Jekyll … marshalled her wide knowledge and tasteful mastery of the best horticulture into an ordered array of facts and suggestions that have been of infinite assistance to thousands of amateur garden makers and maintainers.' In turn, Jekyll praised Tipping's considerable skills as a gardener shown in each of the three properties he developed, Mathern Palace, Mounton House, and High Glanau in Monmouthshire.

Top: *Edward Hudson (1858–1936), proprietor of* Country Life *and longtime admirer of Gertrude Jekyll and Edwin Lutyens.*

Above: *The miniature Lutyens and Jekyll garden for the Queen's Dolls' House, now on display at Windsor Castle.*

Jekyll also shared the predilection of Lawrence Weaver, who was appointed architectural editor of *Country Life* in 1910, for smaller, more vernacular houses, which he promoted in the magazine – unlike Tipping who favoured the larger manor houses. Weaver wrote hundreds of articles about small country houses designed by many of the architects with whom Jekyll collaborated on gardens. Perhaps the most endearing publication he edited was *The Book of the Queen's Dolls' House* (1924), which included a miniature Lutyens and Jekyll garden, replete with bench, planters, climbers, and box-edged parterres.

In addition to writers, Hudson's other stroke of genius was discovering Charles Latham, whose sublime full-plate photographs of houses and gardens from 1898 until his death in 1912 set *Country Life* apart from all the other publications of the day. Although he is largely unknown today, Latham produced an unparalleled record of Edwardian country life at its best and one of his first assignments was Munstead Wood, where he managed to capture the essence of Jekyll's woodland creation unlike any subsequent photographer.

Around the time that Jekyll began contributing to *Country Life*, Hudson founded Country Life Books, a book-publishing

venture that capitalized on the photographs of Latham published in the magazine. *Gardens Old and New* (edited by John Leyland and later Avray Tipping), *The Gardens of Italy*, *In English Homes* (edited by Tipping), and *Garden Ornament* (edited by Jekyll and Hussey) are examples of these sumptuous volumes. They also published some of Jekyll's more practical books, such as *Lilies for English Gardens* (1901), *Wall and Water Gardens* (1901), *Roses for English Gardens* (1902), *Flower Decoration in the House* (1907), and *Annuals and Biennials* (1916).

During her lifetime, Jekyll was known primarily as a writer and not as a garden designer. It was not until the publication of Francis Jekyll's biography of his aunt in 1934 that the full extent of her private design commissions was revealed to those outside her circle. Even though some of her gardens with Lutyens were published in *Country Life*, oddly her name was rarely mentioned. No one knows for certain exactly how many gardens she actually designed or advised on. There are records for about two hundred and fifty projects in her archives at the University of California at Berkeley, but Francis Jekyll lists three hundred and forty commissions. No doubt some represented brief advice, while others, especially those she did for Lutyens, entailed dozens of drawings

Top right: Country Life's *architectural writer H. Avray Tipping (1855–1933) in his garden during tulip time at Mathern Palace, Monmouthshire.*

Above: *Portrait of Sir Edwin Lutyens (1869–1944), painted by Meredith Frampton in 1933.*

and plant lists. Few of her gardens survive in any recognizable form today, for they were designed during an era when trained gardeners were readily available. They were an expensive luxury affordable only by the 'new rich' who had made their fortunes in manufacturing or trade. Jekyll championed the smaller country house garden, designed in collaboration with the homeowner and the architect, and maintained by knowledgeable staff.

Garden design was not a youthful ambition of Jekyll's – she only took it up after abandoning some of her earlier activities due to the onset of myopia. She was already a well-known gardening authority when she began working with Lutyens around 1900, but it was probably her nursery at Munstead Wood that led her to designing gardens in the first place. This was an activity that she genuinely enjoyed, although there were some exasperating moments when clients changed

their minds or were tardy in paying for plants. One curious aspect of her success as a garden designer is that she rarely travelled to any of the sites involved, especially after the early 1900s, and relied mainly on information from the clients. This worked well with gardens in south-east England, where the climate was similar to that of Munstead Wood, but became a problem when she worked in Yorkshire and elsewhere in the north. Her familiarity with local plants and climates served her best in Surrey, where most of her gardens lie.

Whether working with Lutyens or other architects or even on her own, Jekyll's methods were always the same. From a site plan supplied by the client or the engineer, she prepared a general plan showing the basic layout of the garden, with proposed beds and features clearly keyed in with letters and numbers marked in red. From there she would progress to more detailed plans, usually on tracing paper, initially supplied by Lutyens, accompanied by exhaustive plant lists. In many cases Jekyll supplied plants directly from her nursery at Munstead Wood or from other sources, which she carefully listed in a set of notebooks now kept at the

Left: *The rotunda pool at Hestercombe, Somerset, one of Lutyens and Jekyll's most glorious collaborations.*

Below: Country Life *photographer Charles Latham's iconic view of Munstead Wood from the woodland, around 1900, shortly after the house was built.*

Godalming Museum. Those plants that she could not supply were often crossed off in another colour of pencil. Because she rarely visited the gardens, she always requested a survey plan and, if practical, samples of soil and stone. In later projects she sometimes worked with photographs supplied by her clients.

In her work with Lutyens, there were often notes and sketches on the sets of plans that went back and forth between them before the final scheme took shape. Lutyens, of course, saw to it that she was paid for her design services, although information about this aspect of her life is sketchy. In general the gardens she designed on her own were apt to be less architectural in layout than those she designed with Lutyens, which photographed so well for *Country Life*. She continued designing gardens until just before her death, although in her later years she confined her work to flower borders alone rather than to layouts. Even as she grew older and blinder, she could design these borders from memory based on her extensive knowledge of plants and their characteristics.

Jekyll's experience as a garden designer gave her a sense of what was appropriate or inappropriate within the garden. In *Gardens for Small Country Houses* and *Garden Ornament*, she provided examples of some of the best features for gardens, such as pergolas, benches, pools, sculptural ornament, and garden houses, which served to enhance the overall design of the garden, as well as reflect the architectural character of the house. She favoured all styles and approaches, from Harold Peto's elaborate pergolas to the rustic stone walls and whimsical dovecotes of the Cotswold group of designers. In her books and articles, she was never shy in criticizing something that was inappropriate or just plain silly, such as too much ivy covering an interesting building.

*   *   *

Jekyll lived her life to the fullest by restricting her activities to Munstead Wood, where she could quietly write, oversee her gardens, and entertain close friends. She had a rather modest income, especially after the First World War, and entertained infrequently. Her books and articles brought her unwanted attention and she had to beg well-meaning visitors not to come to Munstead Wood, but instead to read her books. As she grew older she became more reclusive and only welcomed old friends, such as Logan Pearsall Smith, Lutyens, and Harold Falkner. She wrote to Ellen Willmott that she found it frustrating not being able to do all the little things about the garden that need to be done and not to be able to walk in her garden. Both Willmott and the ninety-four year old William Robinson were among those who attended her funeral in December 1932, and her old friend Lutyens designed her gravestone, simply inscribed: 'Artist, Gardener, Craftswoman'. The example of Munstead Wood, her writings, and her incomparable flower borders continue to inspire designers and gardeners today. Lanning Roper, writing in *Country Life* in 1967, explained in part why Jekyll made no plans to preserve her home and garden. He wrote, 'A garden is a picture painted with flowers and foliage. Each year and each season there is a slightly different picture, but when the painter is gone the picture may easily alter … until it becomes a bad reproduction.' But Jekyll's garden and her ideas about garden design live on in her books and articles.

Gertrude Jekyll strolling in her spring garden at Munstead Wood in 1918
when she was eighty years old.

Home and Garden

....

*"My own little
new-built house
is so restful,
so satisfying
[and] so kindly
sympathetic."*

....

Munstead Wood, Jekyll's celebrated home in Surrey, was where her inimitable planting style blossomed, based on her horticultural skills combined with her art studies, and where she gave equal consideration to naturalistic gardening as espoused by William Robinson. At Munstead Wood, Jekyll created an idyllic melding of house and garden. From each window of the house there was a particular view of the garden and from the garden there were carefully composed vistas of the house. The legendary house was the creation of the gifted, but fledgling architect, Edwin Lutyens, who interpreted her ideas and learned much about architecture in the process.

As Jekyll confides in *Home and Garden* (1900), 'the building of the house was done in the happiest way possible, a perfect understanding existing between the architect, the builder, and the proprietor.' *Country Life*'s gardens editor wrote in 1900 that he did 'not hesitate to say that this modestly beautiful house, its wood, [and] its garden are clearly destined to become classical.' Twenty-five years later, Avray Tipping wrote in *English Gardens* that at Munstead Wood 'every glade and clearing has become a lovely picture, a gratifying surprise … and everywhere there is composition. The wood approaches the border area or billows on to the lawn without intrusion or abruptness. All is suave and engaging, all is friendly and beautiful. It is a home of undisputed peace.'

As Munstead Wood became familiar through Jekyll's books and articles, people from around the world yearned to see it firsthand. Although she welcomed like-minded gardeners and longtime friends, she claimed eyesight problems, fatigue, and pressing deadlines to all others; 'As a would-be quiet worker', she pleaded to be allowed peace and privacy. She lived quietly at Munstead Wood for thirty-five years, from October 1897, when she moved into her new house, until her death in December 1932, during which time she designed several hundred gardens, wrote nearly one thousand magazine articles and a dozen or so books, and also practised numerous crafts and operated a successful nursery. Although most of

The fern walk is one of several paths that meander through the woodland, each with a different character.

the gardens she designed for clients have disappeared, the articles and books which were based on her experiences at Munstead Wood continue to inspire gardeners today. Fortunately the house and grounds survive in excellent form.

During the years she was living with her mother at Munstead House, Jekyll was undoubtedly dreaming of the house and garden she might have some day. Her brother Herbert would inherit Munstead House after their mother's death in 1895, but a more pressing concern for Jekyll at the time was that she was running out of garden space for her expanding horticultural experiments. Around 1883, the family purchased a tract of land nearby for her to develop, which she described in *Gardens for Small Country Houses* as 'fifteen acres of the poorest possible soil, sloping a little down towards the north [with] a thin skin of peaty earth on the upper part.' There was a natural growth of heath, whortleberry, and bracken growing where a wood of Scots fir had been cut down in the 1870s. A chestnut grove stood in the central portion, where she would eventually build her house, and below that, a poor, sandy field that she later turned into her working gardens. 'These were the conditions that had to be considered and adapted as well as might be to the making of a garden,' she observed.

As Jekyll details in her books and articles, she promptly set out to organize the grounds, keeping some of the natural groupings of trees and shrubs, while thinning out others. She began by creating a series of paths through the woodlands, each with a distinct character. A wide grass walk, nearly 400 feet long and broad enough for two people to walk side by side, was flanked by carefully chosen groups of rhododendrons – pink tones in the foreground and white-flowering types where the woodland became denser and the shade deepened. She referred to this walk as the 'most precious possession' because it gave 'illusions of distance and mystery' and was 'full of charm'. Another walk meandered through the heather; wild ferns, bracken, and lilies bordered some of the smaller, more naturalistic-looking paths, each one of which provided a vista to the house.

After establishing the woodland gardens, she turned her attention to ornamental gardening by creating a series of 'pictures'. Her expertise with seasonal gardens and borders, which was one of the hallmarks of her style of gardening, is fully explained and illustrated in her book *Colour in the Flower Garden* (1908), which, despite its title, has little to do with the subject of colour. One of her primary considerations, however, was the inseparability of house and garden. In the normal course of events, the house and garden would have

been designed together, but at Munstead Wood most of the gardens had been laid out before the house was built. As the architect Robert Lorimer said when he visited in 1897, just six days after she moved into her new home, she had laid out all the gardens first and had 'left a hole in the centre of the ground for the house.' Jekyll later acknowledged that there was no definite plan for the garden and as a result there were many awkward angles that needed to be reconciled when the house was eventually built. 'Various parts [of the garden] were taken in hand at different times and treated on their individual merits, and the whole afterwards reconciled,' she explained.

Around 1895, Jekyll created one of the garden's most memorable features: the main border of hardy flowers, 14 feet

Right: *The south façade of Munstead Wood with pink China roses on the terrace outside the sitting room windows; gentle steps lead up to the lawn and woodland beyond.*

Below: *The main sitting room with low ceilings framed with massive beams of oak. The deeply hooded sandstone fireplace was designed by Jekyll.*

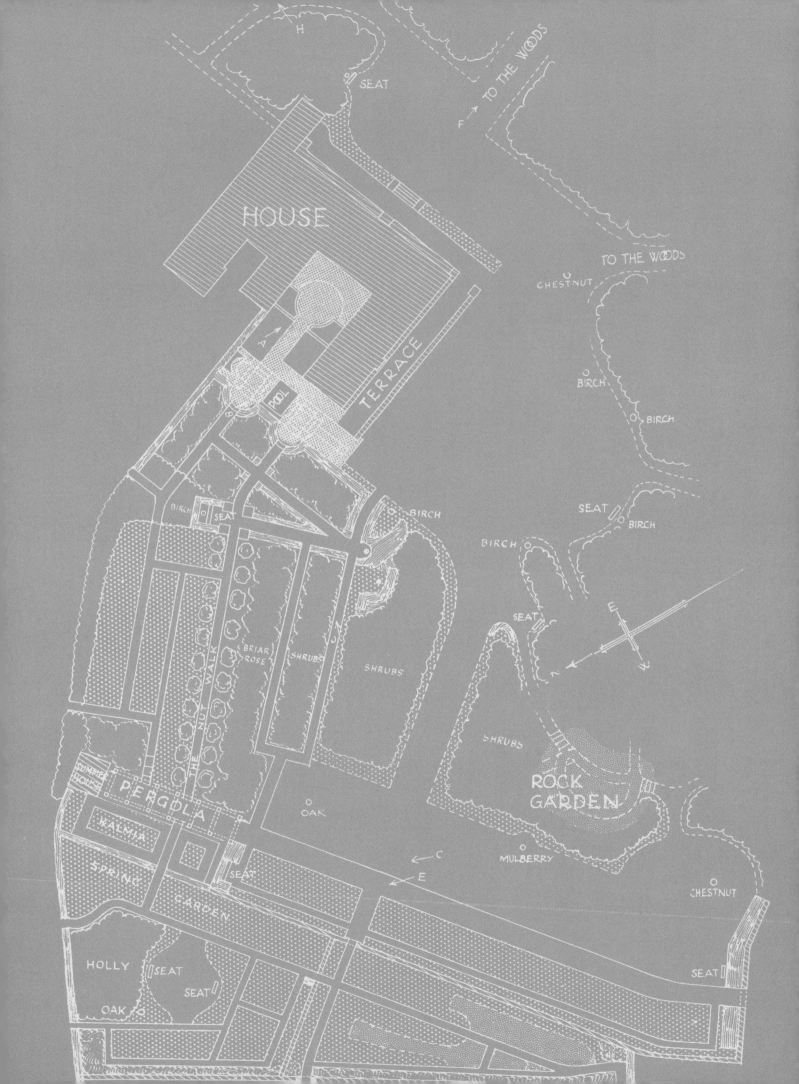

Rare autochromes of the gardens around 1912.

(top left): *The grey garden with masses of grey foliage and white flowers.*

(top right): *The iris and lupin border with the weather-boarded loft in the distance.*

(middle right): *The September aster border in the kitchen garden.*

(below left): *The spring garden with* Euphorbia characias wulfenii *in the corner.*

(below right): *The main flower border.*

wide and 180 feet long, and backed by a high sandstone wall which legend has she built herself. To make such a plan, allowing for a succession of bloom from June through October, was no easy task; it evolved from years of prior experience at Munstead House. In her own words she describes her intention in the plantings: 'The border has a definite colour scheme; at the two ends blue, white and palest yellow, with grey foliage; and purple, white and pink, also with grey foliage, respectively; the colour then advancing from both ends by yellow and orange to the middle glory of strongest reds.' Often imitated, but rarely replicated, this border was a triumph of artful colour planning. Jekyll's black-and-white photographs show the interplay of forms and textures, but some rare autochromes taken by *Country Life* around 1912 show the actual arrangement of the colours. The intricate and complex colour scheme is based on harmonious colour relationships and was perhaps inspired by one of J. M. W. Turner's paintings, such as *The Fighting Téméraire*, which Jekyll had copied in her youth. Once she had settled on the scheme for the border, it remained unchanged for years, with the exception of the duration of the First World War when she used it to grow vegetables.

Later on she developed other colour borders, such as those in the spring garden behind the wall and a dazzling garden of summer flowers consisting mainly of reds, yellows, and purples. In each case she used bold groups of yuccas or euphorbias to add striking foliage at the ends of the borders or to mark cross-paths to other areas of the garden. The spring garden, first laid out in the early 1890s, was one of her favourite parts of Munstead Wood. It was 'wholly devoted to plants that bloom in April or May' and was not part of the main summer border on the other side of the wall. The colour scheme was muted, beginning with drifts of pale yellow daffodils, primroses, and iris, leading to deeper tones of purple wallflowers and tulips. Orange and scarlet tulips were reserved for areas backed by a deep green yew hedge. The garden of summer flowers, which replaced an earlier peony garden, was composed of brilliantly coloured dahlias, cannas, geraniums, African marigolds, and deep purple heliotropes,

Above: *The main border of the spring garden, with Morello cherries on the wall and drifts of spring flowers ranging from pale tones in the foreground to deeper tones in the back.*

Opposite (left): *The tank garden outside Jekyll's workshop door. Pots of Francoa ramosa line the terrace above the pool, with George Leslie's lion masque nestled among the ferns.*
(right): *Gertrude Jekyll strolling in her spring garden in 1918, a photograph taken by* Country Life *gardens editor Herbert Cowley.*

Overleaf: *The square water tank connects the north court of the house with two garden paths. Clipped globes of boxwood and a millstone add notes of formality.*

edged with variegated mint and golden feather feverfew. The use of ordinary bedding annuals such as these often surprised visitors, who expected something more rarified, but Jekyll remarked that it was not the plant's fault that they were often used 'in a dull or even stupid way.'

In addition to flower borders, there were borders for various autumn shrubs, briar roses, and asters. The most famous of all was her Michaelmas daisy border, described in 1900 by *Country Life*'s gardens editor E. T. Cook as 'tumbling waves of purple, and lilac, and palest lavender, and white [and] in front of them is a broad edging of white pinks.' There were actually two aster borders, one for the earlier September-blooming varieties in her kitchen gardens and another dedicated to later-blooming varieties not far from the house. Some of these borders were famously painted by Helen Allingham, the watercolour artist, who lived nearby and who specialized in paintings of tumbledown Surrey cottages, and by George Elgood, a well-known garden painter and Jekyll's co-author of *Some English Gardens*. A special area reserved for late spring flowers later became a rock garden as the surrounding shrubs matured. The hub of the garden, however, was the nursery and kitchen gardens, which visitors rarely saw. Here she had beds for pansies, China

asters, irises, lupins, daffodils, and lily-of-the-valley, as well as special borders dedicated to purple, white, and pink flowers with grey foliage that complemented the old grey barn building. This is where she kept the nursery stock that she used for harvesting seed or providing plants for her design commissions. After her house and other buildings were in place, she continued to add new garden areas and revise old ones.

All the while she was working on her gardens Jekyll was envisioning the house that she would one day build, one that was quite different from her mother's. Her fascination with the domestic architecture and country traditions of West Surrey played a role in its design. Sketchbooks, full of details for buildings observed on her travels through the local countryside and abroad, provided more ideas. Her architectural leanings were in sympathy with Ruskin's call for truth to nature and sincerity in buildings, and her ideas about interior design were inspired by William Morris's home in Bexleyheath, known as Red House, which had bare, whitewashed plaster walls and plain oak trim. In her own neighbourhood she admired old half-timbered manor houses and picturesque rural cottages, some of which she wrote about in her book *Old West Surrey* (1904). She also revelled in local building

customs and the country craftsmen who built cottages in the vernacular style.

After first meeting Jekyll in May 1889, Edwin Lutyens, the young architect from the nearby village of Thursley, quickly fell under her spell and soon they were scouring the Surrey countryside together looking at old buildings. Lutyens, who was barely twenty years old and fresh from Sir Ernest George's architectural practice in London, had recently received his first important commission, for Crooksbury House in Farnham, and modestly asked his new friend for advice on garden design. Lutyens's formative ideas about architecture and passion for vernacular buildings would soon find expression in the building of Munstead Wood. There were animated discussions and many discarded schemes before they hit on the final form of the house, but before it was built, Lutyens was occupied with designing two small cottages on her property. His first proposal for the house in 1892 was for a whitewashed villa, which was quite unsuited to his client's wishes. She sent him back to the

drawing board and later that year he produced a design for a small tile-hung cottage known as The Hut, which was built in 1893. The following year he built a half-timbered cottage at the far corner of the property for her gardener, as well as a small, elevated gazebo where two walls came together and served as a place to watch storms.

For the next year or so Jekyll developed gardens for these cottages: a June-blooming flower garden for The Hut and fruit gardens and an orchard for the gardener's cottage. After her mother's death in July 1895, Jekyll moved into The Hut, where she had already established her workshops, and lived here while her house was under construction.

The house that she had been thinking about for years soon began to take form. 'It does not stare with newness,' she wrote in *Home and Garden*, and 'there is nothing sham-old

Above: *The half-timbered upstairs corridor overlooks the shady north court, with a classic Lutyens bench tucked beneath the overhang.*

Right: Choisya ternata *frames the archway leading from the spring garden to the lawn.*

about it.' It was built of English oak and local honey-coloured sandstone. There were 'no random choosings from the iron-monger's pattern-book' and nothing 'poky or screwy or ill-lighted'. The proportions were perfect and it was just what she wanted, a 'small house with plenty of room in it.' While living in The Hut, a mere 80 yards from the construction site, she could listen to the sounds of the house being built by local craftsmen. She delighted in the 'dull slither' of the moist mortar as it was laid on the brick, the 'melodious scream' of the plane against board, and the 'beating of the cow-hair' as it was mixed with the wall plaster.

Lutyens's design married a small Tudor-style manor house with his own interpretation of local vernacular style. Munstead Wood, both inside and out, embodied all the principles espoused by the Arts and Crafts movement, especially honesty in building and simplicity of design. In *Home and Garden*, she gave Lutyens full credit for the success of

Left: Laburnum anagyroides *in its spring glory on the lawn at Munstead Wood.*
Below: *The main flower border stretches for nearly 200 feet and is sheltered by a high sandstone wall; the colours ranged from pale tones to strong reds and yellows.*

the design. The house was simple, elegant, and comfortable, but it was rather large and expensive (it cost almost £4,000 in 1897) for a single woman. It had a generously-sized long, low sitting room, workshops, storerooms, a service wing, bed-rooms, and three guest rooms, although she rarely entertained overnight guests. Lutyens placed the house on an east-west axis, with a south-facing terrace overlooking the lawn at the edge of the woodland and a shady north court nestled between the two wings of the house. Upstairs, a long oak gallery lined with cupboards filled with her collections, overlooked the courtyard below.

Lutyens's role in planning the gardens at Munstead Wood was minimal, but he did have to contend with them when it came to positioning the house and terraces, which resulted in the 'awkward angles'. The small paved courtyard on the north side, in fact, was the only portion of the garden scheme with a definite plan. The pairs of low steps leading up to the courtyard from the garden, and the tiny square water tank between them, provide a dissonant, formal note in an other-wise informal garden. The most successful aspect of linking

the house and grounds was the small footpath leading from the lane to the house, as there was no carriage drive sweeping up to the front door, as one might have expected. 'I like the approach to a house to be as quiet and modest as possible, and in this case I wanted it to tell its own story as the way in to a small dwelling standing in wooded ground.' In her later collaborations with Lutyens, Jekyll always made the entrance plantings as restrained as possible and reserved the more floriferous components to the areas behind the house.

The hall and south terrace were centred on the Green Wood Walk laid out fifteen years earlier; where it met the lawn there were groups of silver birch mingling with the rhododendrons. From the terrace one could see large sweeps of daffodils growing in the old smugglers' tracks and in a broad clearing in the centre of the woodland there were brilliantly coloured Ghent hybrid azaleas. Along the south terrace Jekyll planted masses of rosemary and pink China roses, with a grape vine trained on the wall. The courtyard on the north side was wreathed in *Clematis montana* and decorated with pots filled with hostas, lilies, and ferns. Pots also lined the edge of the tank garden, with lilies and cannas reflecting into the pool. Each of the paths in the ornamental gardens to the west was flanked by borders, which provided a succession of bloom as well as unique vistas of the house. E. T. Cook wrote in *Gardens Old and New* that 'it is a garden of natural character [that depends] for its charm upon the abundant use of the glories of the flower world,' but it is Charles Latham's dreamy photographs of 1900 that truly show this unusual house in its magical woodland setting, where it seems to just grow out of the ground.

Jekyll's gardens gave her ample subject matter for the hundreds of garden notes she wrote for over thirty years for *Country Life* in addition to her books. In her articles published prior to the First World War, she supplied most of the pictures herself, but after that she relied on photographs taken by Herbert Cowley, who became *Country Life*'s gardens editor after the departure of Cook in 1911. Cowley, who was a frequent guest at Munstead Wood, snapped the famous picture of Jekyll strolling in her spring garden in 1918. He also served as editor of *The Garden* and *Gardening Illustrated* around the same time, which explains the duplication of numerous articles in these publications.

Throughout the 1910s and 1920s, Jekyll wrote monthly columns for *Country Life*'s 'In the Garden' feature, and with

Previous pages: *Gertrude Jekyll's brilliantly coloured Ghent hybrid azaleas are one of the glories of Munstead Wood.*

Right: *Mature rhododendrons flank the Green Wood Walk, the principal woodland path linking house and garden, which Jekyll described as her most precious possession.*

few exceptions they were about borders in her kitchen gardens rather than the ornamental gardens surrounding the house, indicating where her gardening energies lay at that time. One of her constant themes was the use of grey foliage: 'To those who regard their gardens as giving opportunities of displaying a series of pictures of plant beauty … the use of grey foliage with the accompaniment of suitable flowers is one of the most valuable,' she wrote in 1921. Ever the artist, she suggested that 'in walking through a garden, after passing some groups of gorgeous red and orange, it is an extraordinary relief and pleasure to the eye to come to a place of tender colouring set in a ground of grey.' In another article she suggested that purple, lilac, and pink flowers were especially suited for grouping with grey, provided there was a

Above: A magnificent Cercis siliquastrum *(Judas tree) in the annual garden adjacent to the spring garden.*

Left: Jekyll's spring garden is tucked behind the wall of the main flower border; Viburnum opulus *frames the doorway from the lawn.*

Overleaf: A riot of lupins and other spring-blooming plants in the spring garden, with Munstead Quadrangle in the distance.

sprinkling of white blossoms. Most of the borders she described in her articles were in separate areas surrounding a picturesque weather-boarded loft that Lutyens had concocted from an old barn that was about to be demolished. The loft's pale grey-toned boards provided the perfect backdrop for the grey foliage borders.

The end of the First World War brought financial hardship to Jekyll, who was by then in her seventies and growing more reclusive. It affected the level of maintenance in her gardens, which her earnings from *Country Life* helped support. Before that she may have lived beyond her means, with a large staff, including a head gardener and two under-gardeners. Her nursery sales also helped defray expenses, but in the end she made few improvements to the house or garden. At the time of her death in 1932, the shrubberies around the house were considerably overgrown, and most were later cleared so that an entrance drive could be added. By then the house and garden were considered an anachronism, which together with the dispersal of her estate and the breaking up of the property

in 1948 seemed to spell doom. Her professional papers found a good home at the University of California at Berkeley, after they were purchased by the American landscape architect Beatrix Farrand, who was an early admirer of Jekyll's and had initially visited Munstead Wood in 1895.

The house and woodland gardens survive in excellent condition, and separate parcels, all still privately owned, include The Hut, the gardener's cottage, and the kitchen gardens (now known as Munstead Quadrangle). Jekyll's legacy lies primarily in the books and articles she wrote about Munstead Wood and the photographic record by Charles Latham, Herbert Cowley, and Jekyll herself.

Left: *The gate in the hedge connects the spring garden with Jekyll's former kitchen gardens.*

This page (right): *Jekyll's famous 'Munstead bunch' primroses, first discovered in a cottage garden in 1873, still thrive today among the hellebores.*

(below): *Munstead Quadrangle, the weather-boarded loft where Jekyll stored seeds and nursery stock.*

Overleaf: *Munstead Wood remains one of the finest examples of Lutyens's Surrey-vernacular style.*

Gardens Old and New

. . . .

*"There is no
problem before the
architect and
garden designer
more difficult, and
at the same time
more attractive,
than is presented in
small sites."*

. . . .

*Owlpen Manor, an early Tudor manor house
set in the Cotswold hills.*

Jekyll's earliest articles, beginning in the early 1880s, were primarily focused on the finer points of horticulture and botany and it wasn't until after her first books were published that she began to reveal her expert knowledge of garden history and the design lessons that could be learned from it. As her range of subjects widened it became increasingly apparent that she was an unusually astute critic of gardens both old and new.

For the most part, her personal ideas about garden design were informed by her love of old English manor house gardens, such as St. Catherine's Court, Owlpen Manor, Cleeve Prior Manor, and numerous other places tucked away in remote corners of England.

Many of these manor house gardens were featured in *Country Life* articles, and later gathered into the three-volume folio, *Gardens Old and New*. Whether these gardens were grand in size or more intimately scaled, it was their simple compartmental arrangement and connection to the house and surrounding landscape that she took as her guide for designing new gardens. She admired long, broad terraces; simple, yet dramatic stairways connecting the various levels; and the judicious use of evergreens and foliage. Although she shared Reginald Blomfield's admiration for the formal arrangement of old manor house gardens and their traditional ornament, such as sundials and urns, she raised the bar considerably by introducing richly planted flower borders and massive sweeps of ornamental shrubs and climbing vines to further link house and garden.

When *Gardens Old and New* first appeared in 1901, the editor acknowledged the growing appreciation of the relationship between houses and gardens. The controversies lay in how to achieve this necessary relationship. 'Some have demanded harmony, others contrast. There are those who look upon gardening as merely a form of architecture, maintaining that a garden is really the extension of the house into its surroundings, [while others] consider gardening as the approach of wild Nature, subjected and glorified, to the dwelling-place.' The battle lines were drawn between the opposing viewpoints of architects and gardeners, but Jekyll sensibly took the middle ground by melding the best of both 'old' and 'new.'

As Jekyll's appreciation of architecture and construction methods grew, she had her favourite architects when it came to laudable new gardens designed and built on old models. Among them she reserved the highest praise for the work of H. Inigo Triggs, H. Avray Tipping, Charles E. Mallows, Thackeray Turner, Walter Brierley, and, of course, Edwin Lutyens. The work of all these architects was featured in much detail in *Gardens for Small Country Houses*, as well as in individual articles by her co-author Lawrence Weaver and other writers for *Country Life*.

Above right: *A rare photograph of a Victorian turf stairway at St Catherine's Court, Somerset.*

Left: *A fine Jacobean staircase flanked by sentinel yews at St. Catherine's Court.*

St. Catherine's Court, Somerset

Jekyll's earliest signed piece about an historical garden, St. Catherine's Court in Somerset, appeared in 1906. Although an earlier article by another writer had appeared in 1898, and was included in the initial volume of *Gardens Old and New* in 1901, *Country Life* undoubtedly felt the garden merited a new assessment by their resident garden authority. It also presented an opportunity for new pictures by Charles Latham. In many ways, Jekyll's article summed up all her basic tenets of timeless design considerations while revealing some of the pet peeves she elaborated on in later articles and books. The opening words of her article – 'Many are the beautiful houses and gardens in the county of Somerset, but there is hardly one within its own borders, or, indeed, within the length and breadth of England, whose charm of ancient beauty and of lovely, restful pleasure-ground, can rival that of this delightful place' – immediately drew the reader to the exceptional quality of the property. She maintained that it was a purely English garden, not one that strived after Italian mannerism as seen in so many gardens attached to fine English houses.

Jekyll admired the fine Jacobean garden staircase flanked by sentinel yews that was added in the seventeenth century when improvements were made to the Tudor manor house. Terrace after terrace rises up to the house and its adjacent church. 'The eye enjoys the visible prospect, and the mind roves with keen expectancy, in joyful anticipation of the many delights that will probably be found to right and left on each successive level,' she observed. The main flower garden is filled with lavender and lupins, and another border at the foot of the wall is 'sufficiently clothed, but not smothered, with climbing plants.' A long bowling green on an upper level has narrow borders, and above the wall is a 'mighty hedge of yew.' Seen from above, 'this massive hedge of solid verdure forms a noble frame or setting to the garden picture [and] the hedge is wisely placed, for what it bounds and

Above: *Jekyll considered St. Catherine's Court one of the most delightful houses and gardens in Somerset.*

Right: *Charles Latham's photograph of 1906 captures Jekyll's praise for the adaptability of the English ways of gardening; the ancient manor house and church provide the perfect setting for a timeless garden.*

encloses is quite enough for any one garden picture.' Echoing William Robinson, she continued: 'The lawn is flanked on either side by Irish yews, trimmed to a shape. Whether it is ever desirable to clip Irish yews is very doubtful. They will only clip into one form, and that is not a graceful one, whereas their own shape is a good one.'

'St. Catherine's Court gives ample evidence of the adaptability of our English ways of gardening. Within the last quarter of a century we … have acquired a yet higher perception of all that our gardens can do for us… . It may be said that in a place like this gardening is easy. The main lines of it are here and unalterable; the permanent features – hill, valley, woodland, terraces and noble flights of stairs – these are all present, and only waiting to be suitably and sufficiently clothed and adorned. But it should be done just rightly, for there are numberless ways of going wrong.' In her delightfully restrained plea for simplicity, she also waved the

banner for selecting plants carefully: 'It helps to keep in mind colour relations between plants and shrubs, and to work out the groupings accordingly, and to remember that no one portion of the garden can be in full beauty for the whole year.' 'A garden that so amply possesses the magic of the ancient charm is best without the off-shoots or adjuncts that are quite reasonable in places of modern make… . It does not want an alpine garden, or a water garden, or a pergola garden, or a Japanese garden,' she admonished. Her final recommendation was that it was time to end 'the worship of the specimen conifer, whose presence has destroyed the character of many a fine old garden.' Happily, she said, 'the vandalisms of the last generation are no longer practical … and fine old places are recovering their ancient charm.'

Owlpen Manor, Gloucestershire

Owlpen Manor, a modest, early Tudor manor house set in a deep valley under the Cotswold hills, near Uley, is a perfect example of the sympathetic arrangement of a site in the natural conditions of its surroundings. Possibly one of the oldest formal gardens in England, Owlpen has long been the object of garden pilgrims from Jekyll to Vita Sackville-West ('a dream') and Sir Geoffrey Jellicoe ('remote' and 'mysterious'). In more recent years Owlpen has been recognized not only for its romantic situation, but also as a splendid example of the unusually sensitive repair undertaken by the Arts and Crafts architect, Norman Jewson. Jewson, who recognized the Sleeping Beauty in 1925, and succeeded in buying it at auction, spent two years restoring it, inside and out, to its former glory. The present owners continue to care for this ancient house and have recently restored some of the garden features.

In *Gardens for Small Country Houses*, Jekyll praised the 'wealth of incident crowded into an area of little more than half an acre' and revelled in the modesty with which the house 'nestles against the hillside and seeks to hide itself amidst regiments of yews.' She praised the skill in planting, which emphasized the level changes between the succeeding terraces. The small garden, which begins on the high slope above the house, drops down 25 feet in a sequence of five terraces (the house is on the second terrace). Adjacent to the house is a small compartment of well-established ornamental yews, and further down the slope is an unusual rectangular 'yew parlour' (sometimes called 'the ball room'), enclosed

Above: *Owlpen Manor is renowned for its romantic setting in which the manor house nestles comfortably against the hillside in a deep valley.*

Right: *A gentle garden path, lined with ancient yews, offers a rare glimpse of the old house on one of the upper terraces.*

with high walls of yew then 25-feet high and still extant today. The main path, flanked by yews on both sides, descends from the south side of the house down to the lowest terrace and terminates with an attractive eighteenth-century gateway and semicircular steps leading down to the surrounding landscape, with a ha-ha separating the property from the fields beyond.

Tipping, writing in 1906, commended the garden for its individuality and the wealth of flowering plants in and among the old yews. 'There is surely an enduring charm in such a garden … a pleasaunce of terraces and clipped yews, of woodland and distant views – a true old garden of England.' And Hussey, who first visited Owlpen in 1925 and reckoned that the garden's distinctive yews had originally been planted around 1710, described it as a 'simple yet exquisite little house in an incomparably romantic situation.' In many ways Owlpen exemplified the ideal garden in Jekyll's mind's eye, one which could be adapted to many diverse situations. Simplicity, charm, individuality, and sympathy for the site were the timeless components of any good design.

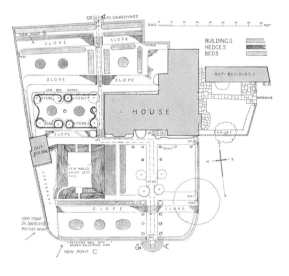

Majestic clipped yews enclosed by low boxwood edging on one of the steep terraces overlooking the valley beyond.

Cleeve Prior Manor, Worcestershire

Another equally delightful old manor house and garden that Jekyll admired was Cleeve Prior Manor, located in a remote village in the northern Cotswolds. The seventeenth-century stone manor house and farm buildings were once attached to the Abbey of Evesham, which may account for the excellence of the buildings. 'The old monks were grand constructors, and their structures were not only solid but always beautiful,' Jekyll wrote in *Some English Gardens*. Among those buildings is a large, circular dovecote of stone masonry with a tiled roof, which survives today. These ecclesiastical origins may explain the presence of one of the most extraordinary features

of the farm, the majestic avenue of double yews leading from the small hand-gate on the lane to the front door of the stone house. The yews, of ancient origin, are said to represent the twelve Apostles and the four Evangelists. 'At a little more than halfway of their height each pair stretches out branches to the next, forming a connecting arch, so that the framed garden scene, five times repeated, is visible from right to left,' Jekyll wrote in *Gardens for Small Country Houses*. Hedges of yew with turf alone, she added, 'have an extraordinary quality of repose – of inspiring a sentiment of refreshing contentment.'

Cleeve Prior perfectly exemplifies the old English idea of enclosed space, relying on simple features such as rows of yew set off with green lawn. Jekyll also admired how the garden successfully blended old and modern themes with the inclusion of simple flower beds, memorialized in period

Left: *The large, circular stone dovecote at Cleeve Prior Manor is framed by the yews of ancient origin. Simple flower borders successfully blend old and new garden themes.*

Below: *An elegant hand-gate on the lane leads to the front door of the old manor house.*

paintings by George Elgood. 'How grandly the flowers grow in these old manor and farm gardens! How finely the great masses of bloom compose, and how beautifully they harmonise with the grey of the limestone wall and the wonderful colour of the old tiled roof ... each tile a picture in itself of grey and orange and tenderest pink.' The deep green yews provide a handsome backdrop for brightly coloured flowers from May to September. Informal clusters of dahlias, sunflowers, daisies, lavender, and Michaelmas daisies make an attractive garden picture. Old pot-herbs, such as sage, hyssop, marjoram, savory, and thyme among others, are quite at home in a country garden. Jekyll wrote about the charm of cottage gardens and their plants in *Wood and Garden*: 'They have a simple and tender charm that one may look for in vain in gardens of greater pretension. And the old garden flowers seem to know that there they are seen at their best.'

In the end, Jekyll said there was much to learn in the examples of older farmhouses and buildings throughout England. In addition to architects, anyone who takes 'the pleasant trouble to learn enough about it to understand how and why the buildings were reared' can reap great rewards. 'There is a delightful sense of restfulness about these fine solid buildings [and] there is also a satisfaction in the plain evidence of delight in good craftsmanship, and in the unsparing use of both labour and material.'

Above: *One of Charles Latham's early photographs of Cleeve Prior, showing the east gable of the manor house and simple flower beds in about 1900.*

Left: *The double avenue of yews between the gate and manor house are thought to represent the twelve Apostles and four Evangelists. Their branches form a line of connecting arches.*

Great Tangley Manor, Surrey

Closer to home, it was on one of Jekyll's jaunts in the 1860s that she discovered a neglected old manor house just three miles from her childhood home in Bramley, Surrey. Great Tangley Manor, a moated timber-built house, was then hidden away behind an assortment of old farm buildings in a thicket of wild thorns and elders, and, according to Tipping, a cabbage garden that came right up to the front door. The memory of the romantic house and its overgrown garden lingered for years, and she later admired the work of Wickham Flower, who rescued the property in 1884 and proceeded to clean out the moat, lay out new gardens in the old enclosures, and build a long pergola which crosses the moat and leads to the house. He also hired the architect Philip Webb to refurbish the house and add a sympathetically-inspired library wing for his large collection of books. Jekyll returned in the late 1880s to photograph some of the details of the garden architecture and the landscape, such as the space in front of the house, once the site of an ancient garden and enclosed by old loopholed walls of great thickness, a remnant of earlier times when they were necessary for defence. On one

Top: *The neglected old moat at Great Tangley Manor was cleaned out in the 1880s by Wickham Flower, who added a new pergola which crosses the moat.*

Above: *The architect Philip Webb, who refurbished the old manor house, added a new library wing and the new flower borders replaced an old cabbage garden.*

Opposite (above): *The rock garden, one of the informal gardens beyond the moat, was located in a dell filled with creeping rock-loving plants.*
(below): *The water gardens at Great Tangley were 'a paradise for flower-lovers'.*

of her trips to Great Tangley she brought along Lutyens, who recast the loophole detail in the garden walls at Hestercombe and elsewhere, and admired the simple Tudor arched door-way, which reappeared in his design at Millmead.

In 1904, she wrote that the water garden beyond the moat was 'a paradise for flower-lovers', filled with masses of irises, waterlilies, and white calla lilies, which inspired the plantings in the tanks at Hestercombe and Folly Farm, among others. She also admired the bog garden filled with clumps of showy moccasin flowers (*Cypripedium spectabile*), as well as a garden devoted to heaths and 'a capital rock-garden of the best and simplest form.' The rock garden was just one long dell, edged with local stone and 'sheets' of creeping and rock-loving plants. A dense backdrop of shrubby greenery kept it hidden from other parts of the grounds. 'The picture speaks for itself … it tells of a right appreciation of the use of good autumn flowers, in masses large enough to show what the flowers will do for us at their best, but not so large as to become wearisome or monotonous… each open space gives a picture of water and water-plants with garden ground beyond, and, looking a little forward, the picture is varied by the back-ground of roof-mass with a glimpse of the timbered gables of the old house.' In her mind's eye she painted as romantic a picture of Great Tangley as the artists Thomas Hunn, George Elgood, and E. A. Rowe, all of whom did watercolours of the 'new' garden.

Dense shrubbery kept some of the informal gardens hidden from the house, including the 'capital rock-garden', which Jekyll thought was one of the best.

Little Boarhunt, Hampshire

Of all the architects who shared Jekyll's love of architectural history and an affinity for formal principles applied to the art of garden design, Harry Inigo Triggs was one of the best, but his architectural work has been overshadowed by the legacy of his books on formal garden design. Taking a leaf from the pages of Reginald Blomfield's book *The Formal Garden in England* (1892), Triggs published a sumptuous folio in 1902 entitled *Formal Gardens in England and Scotland*, with large-plate photographs by Charles Latham and exceptionally attractive plans of many famous examples from St. Catherine's Court and Monacute House to Hampton Court Palace and Penshurst Place. Other plans, such as those of Earlshall, Barncluith, Stobhall, and other Scottish examples, were executed by L. Rome Guthrie, an architect whose work bears similarity to that of Triggs. The book was a *tour de force* with its distinctive presentation of measured drawings and was followed by *The Art of Garden Design in Italy* (1906) in the same format, and a final volume, *Garden Craft in Europe* (1913), which extends well beyond the borders of England and Italy.

Triggs worked primarily with the Unsworth firm (both father and son) on projects in Hampshire, including Ashford Chace and Sparshold Manor, but it was his own house and garden near Liphook that caught Jekyll's eye. Named Little Boarhunt, presumably because King John once ran a boar through the property, Triggs skilfully converted a small farmhouse and yard into a model of the Arts and Crafts ideal of the intimacy of house and garden. Jekyll singled it out as a good example of the treatment of small sites in *Gardens for Small Country Houses*. '[In] the revival of the right principles of garden design in England during the last twenty years,' she wrote in 1912, 'Mr. Inigo Triggs has taken a leading part.' Little Boarhunt, she thought, 'shows how the qualities that make the beauty of the historic formal gardens may be reproduced in little for houses of moderate size.'

After purchasing the property in 1910, Triggs 'smoothed many banks in the making of his garden' which lies at the edge of an old woodland dell. The drive leading up to the house is bordered with beds of herbaceous plants, instead of 'dull shrubs that too often find a place there.'

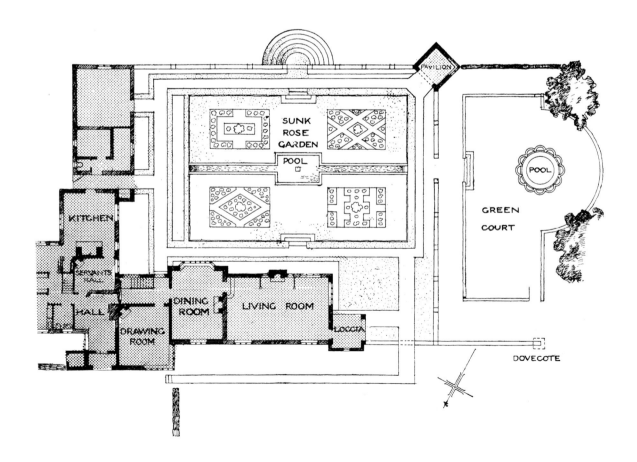

Inigo Triggs's own garden at Little Boarhunt in Hampshire
nestles into the L-shaped small house.

Triggs excavated the farmyard to create a sunken rose garden broken into four beds divided by narrow brick paths set in different designs. A long brick canal with a central rectangular pool runs the length of the sunken garden. It is 'an admirable example of the wealth of interesting detail that can be employed in a small space without creating any feeling of overcrowding.' The retaining walls of rough stone are planted with saxifrages, pinks, and veronicas, with herbaceous borders at the foot of the walls. The stone piers of a pergola that runs along the outer edge of the sunken garden are covered with climbing roses. At the corner opposite the house a small garden pavilion built of brick further serves to enclose the beautiful, yet simple outdoor room. The garden's genius is in the use of common materials, its sense of scale, and delightful features that perfectly complement the old house.

Above: *The stone retaining walls surrounding the rose garden are planted with grey-foliage plants that complement the rose beds.*

Left: *The sunken rose garden consisting of four beds and a long water rill is enclosed by a raised rose-covered pergola with a small garden pavilion in one corner.*

Westbrook, Surrey

This same sensitive use of materials, restraint of design, and appropriateness of scale can be found at Westbrook, a new house in Jekyll's own neighbourhood near Godalming in Surrey. 'When an architect of ripe experience and keen sensibility plans a house and garden for his own home,' Jekyll and Weaver wrote in *Gardens for Small Country Houses*, 'one may look for something more than usually interesting, and in Westbrook one is not disappointed.' Westbrook was the home of the local architect Hugh Thackeray Turner, who was active in the Society for the Protection of Ancient Buildings (SPAB) and shared sympathies for old buildings with William Morris and Philip Webb. But for his own house he wanted something new which embodied the principles of the Arts and Crafts movement, from its use of local sandstone and red roof tiles to the small garden enclosure. Weaver wrote in *Country Life* in 1912 that Westbrook is 'simple [and] unaffected … it shows what can be done by using local materials in a straightforward yet thoughtful fashion [and] no less engaging is the garden setting.' In their book they described the garden in more detail. Whether Jekyll advised on the

garden layout is unknown, but she did supply plants from her nursery.

To create a sense of enclosure, a low, stone garden wall extends along the terrace; perpendicular to that is a walkway lined with pleached lime trees. A summerhouse is placed on the opposite side of the lawn. To the east are kitchen gardens, but the main ornamental gardens lie to the west of the house, where the centrepiece is a circular sunk garden ablaze with midsummer flowers, and other areas devoted to roses and autumn flowers, as well as a delightful enclosed winter garden for bloom from November through April. In their own words, 'the garden to the west of the house abounds in charming surprises. Its various subdivisions are linked together in a simple general design. Each section shows some distinct way of making a garden picture, and each entices onwards to the

Above: *Westbrook, the architect Thackeray Turner's house near Godalming, reflects the principles of the Arts and Crafts movement in its small garden enclosure.*

Opposite (above): *The sunken garden to the west of the house consists of a circular pool surrounded by billowing summer flowers.*
(below): *High clipped hedges enclose the sunken garden with large trees in the distance.*

next by the charm of mystery and the stimulus of pleasant anticipation of something still better to follow.' The various areas are delineated by high clipped hedges, with 'bright blossom showing finely against the background of dark yew.' There is also a heather garden concealed in the shrubbery, a fruit orchard, and areas on the outer edges planted with gorse and broom. A wonderful balance has been achieved with formality and informality, both in the plantings and in the details. There are solid stone walls and arches, yet the paths are sand; there is also a judicious amount of grass. Sheltered seats ensure that the garden can be enjoyed most of the year.

Writing in *Country Life* in 1915, Jekyll reveals more about the garden than she did three years earlier in *Gardens for Small Country Houses*. She laments the problems of gardening in the light, sandy soil of West Surrey, which always needs regular manuring, 'a serious drain on the horticultural exchequer.' But among the compensations are that the soil can be worked year-round and that plants will not be overly vigorous, yet bloom abundantly. She tips her hat to Thackeray Turner for understanding these conditions and for designing a garden in close sympathy for the ways of hardy flowers. She commended his restraint in adorning, not smothering, the stone arch in the wall that separates the inner and outer gardens with roses. 'One of the many pleasures of a garden is the planning and invention of various devices to suit the needs of special plants and places.'

At Westbrook, Turner succeeded on many different levels and won Jekyll's praise as a special artist. The remarkable house is well cared for today and the delightful garden architecture anchors the garden to the house in the best manner of the Arts and Crafts philosophy.

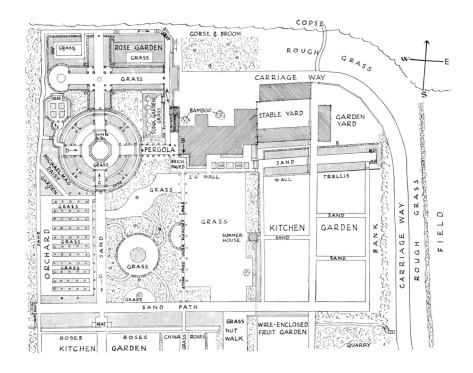

Left: *A walkway lined with pleached lime trees seen from the study window.*

Gardens for
Small Country Houses

....

*"It is upon the
right relation of the
garden to the house
that its value
and the enjoyment
that is to be
derived from it will
largely depend."*

....

*Tigbourne Court, Surrey, Jekyll's quintessential cottage garden
for an early Lutyens house.*

Jekyll's fortuitous meeting with Edwin Lutyens in 1889 not only led to the creation of one of the most famous houses and gardens in the world, but it also gave birth to an extraordinary design partnership that has rarely been rivalled. 'A Lutyens house and a Jekyll garden' became the catchphrase among the wealthy artistic set, as well as those with social aspirations. The story of this legendary partnership, first presented in Jane Brown's book *Gardens of a Golden Afternoon*, still enthralls lovers of English country houses. Had he not met Jekyll, Lutyens would certainly be remembered as an architectural genius, but those gardens he designed without the benefit of her advice lack spark.

Likewise, Jekyll's reputation as an esteemed horticulturist and writer is legend (and this is how she was remembered upon her death), but her prowess as a garden designer might never have reached its zenith without the opportunities provided by Lutyens. Their mutually beneficial partnership would span forty years and range over more than fifty gardens. Thanks to the incomparable record of Lutyens's architectural career presented in the pages of *Country Life*, there are superb examples of his collaboration with Jekyll, unlike most of her other projects which are largely absent from the magazine.

While Munstead Wood was being designed and built, the friendship between Lutyens and Jekyll quickened and soon she was introducing the young architect to future clients. Lutyens's career soared between 1897 and 1901, when he created some of his most memorable houses in a picturesque Surrey-vernacular style. Among them, Sullingstead (now known as High Hascombe), Orchards, Fulbrook House, Tigbourne Court, and Goddards can be considered the best. From this he progressed to classically-inspired houses, such as Millmead, Little Thakeham, Marsh Court, and lastly, Gledstone Hall. Jekyll's style, on the other hand, proved more static, and even well into the 1920s, when she was most in demand, her design solutions continued to be based on ideas she had formulated while living at Munstead House in the 1880s.

Jekyll's luxurious flower borders at Folly Farm, Berkshire, where Lutyens designed several additions to a former dairy farm.

Lutyens's genius in the creation and manipulation of space and his reliance on geometry resulted in a rigid framework when applied to garden design. In contrast, Jekyll's more informal style was based on lush planting compositions, such as those at Folly Farm. The success of their partnership centred on her ability to offset the crisp edges of lawns, paving, and other architectural features with plantings that gave consideration to colour, texture, and three-dimensionality. The best example of the genius of this partnership is evident at Hestercombe Gardens, where Lutyens's exquisite, if not excessive geometric detailing, is softened with Jekyll's signature plantings, ranging from restrained soft-hued grey-foliage borders against stone walls to sweeps of more brilliantly coloured compositions in the open parterres.

The marriage of these two capabilities – formal geometry and informal texture – came to represent the Arts and Crafts approach to garden making, which was explained in detail in Jekyll and Weaver's *Gardens for Small Country Houses* (1912). This approach proved influential in more complex, later gardens, such as Vita Sackville-West and Harold Nicolson's Sissinghurst Castle.

While Lutyens has been credited in all their projects with providing the general layouts, as well as designs for pergolas, terraces, steps, pools, and other features, he benefited from Jekyll's guidance regarding their suitability and placement in the overall scheme. Their celebrated collaboration is reflected in some of the most brilliant gardens of the early twentieth century.

In contrast to the subtlety of the grounds, one of the most striking areas at Orchards is the large walled kitchen garden, which one can view from the terrace. A grand tile-capped archway, with Lutyens's distinctive radiating bands of tiles between the stones, leads to the walled garden. Double flower borders, ablaze with hollyhocks, sunflowers, phlox, and marigolds, stand out from the carpet of grey foliage, such as *Cineraria maritima*, gypsophila, and santolina. A central tank with a dipping well is festooned with swags of cluster roses. A so-called 'Dutch' garden on the east terrace of the house was an invention of Lutyens rather than a copy of anything from Holland. An exercise in geometry, it has three large semicircular seats that echo the circular steps leading down to the terrace.

In some ways, Orchards is successful because of the way in which the gardens respond to the natural setting. Designed as a whole, rather than piecemeal like Munstead Wood, the gardens incorporate numerous features that would become signatures of their partnership, but none of their later commissions were as simple and satisfying as Orchards. As in the case for many of their early Surrey projects, few architectural and garden plans survive.

Above: *Lutyens's signature semicircular steps connecting the loggia with the gardens make their first appearance at Orchards.*

Right: *Lush double herbaceous borders between the house and the walled kitchen garden.*

Tigbourne Court, Surrey

Described by Pevsner as Lutyens's 'gayest building', Tigbourne Court in Witley, Surrey, provided an opportunity for a different type of garden. The unconventional, three-gabled, front façade and dramatic entry piers, just yards from the busy road, contrast with the more picturesque garden façade. The house of Bargate stone, with joints inlaid with blackstone clippings, was built for Edgar Horne, an architectural fancier with a reverence for English domestic architecture. Horne chose to retain an old cottage that stood on the 3-acre property along with mature stands of cypress and yew, but he promptly cleared the languishing orchards of fruit trees to make way for the new house and garden. The house itself has fanciful balconies, loggias, and delicious details that give it a sense of levity. In the gardens, Lutyens added simple paved steps, a seat near the tennis lawn, and a pergola with alternating round and square piers constructed of thin, tile-like brick. The geometrical play of round and square piers would reappear on a grander scale in other projects, such as Deanery Garden and Hestercombe.

The pergola, which was framed by the deep green cypress hedge behind it, was planted with vines and rambling roses with a well underneath. It also served as a shady retreat for the croquet lawn below the house terrace. A line of whimsical bird topiaries along the terrace wall added a note of formality to an otherwise simple garden scheme. Numerous flower borders injected colour into the basically green garden composed of mature trees and shrubs. In some ways, Tigbourne Court is little more than an exquisite cottage garden, although a bit more organized than the picturesque one it replaced.

Above: *Fanciful bird topiaries on the terrace at Tigbourne Court, where Lutyens's picturesque façade overlooks the gardens.*

Opposite (above): *Lutyens's pergola, with alternating square and round piers, served as a shady retreat for the adjacent croquet lawn.*
(below): *The piers and crossbeams of the pergola are heavily planted with vines and rambling roses.*

Le Bois des Moutiers, France

Lutyens's commissions soon spread beyond the confines of Surrey and one of his most imaginative projects took him to an English enclave near Dieppe in Normandy, where he transformed an undistinguished brick house into a Continental version of an English Arts and Crafts house. His client, Guillaume Mallet, was a confirmed Anglophile and probably found Lutyens through Lady Emily Lutyens's aunt, Theresa Earle, whom he knew. Located in Varengeville-sur-Mer, Le Bois des Moutiers is still owned by the same family and one of the few Lutyens's houses to remain in unaltered condition. Beginning in 1898, Lutyens took the original rectangular house and literally buried it beneath stucco. He also extended it, adding a new wing and a large music room with windows facing the sea. In the process, he created an asymmetrical house with unusual elevations, curious windows, and eccentric detailing. The house was furnished throughout with English Arts and Crafts furniture and decorative arts.

The house is approached by a long drive lined with deep herbaceous borders which leads to a circular courtyard in front of a new entrance porch. Along the path in front of the house Lutyens added a brick pergola and a tile-capped

Above: *The tile-capped archway in the garden wall at Le Bois des Moutiers is decorated with radiating bands of tile.*

Right: *The parterre garden between the garden wall and the grand Arts and Crafts style house.*

Overleaf: *A brick path flanked by herbaceous borders leads from the long drive to a circular courtyard at the entrance.*

archway in the garden wall similar to the one at Orchards. In 1904, Jekyll was asked to provide some planting schemes, but Mallet, an avid gardener, had his own ideas and chose to interpret her plans rather loosely.

Today the house is covered in luscious, mature climbers and the grounds running down to the sea have been transformed into an arboretum. The old kitchen garden has been turned into a nursery and the more formal garden rooms surrounding the house are strongly influenced by Jekyll. This is due to the efforts of the Mallets's grandson, Robert Mallet, who infused new life into the extraordinary garden framework following in the footsteps of his father, André Mallet, who rescued the garden from years of neglect after the Second World War and created the Parc des Moutiers. Among the most outstanding features on the estate today are the glades of rhododendrons and Ghent azaleas in the naturalistic gardens, which closely resemble those at Munstead Wood.

Deanery Garden, Berkshire

By 1900 Lutyens and Jekyll hit their stride, although Lutyens had designed several other notable houses, such as Grey Walls in Gullane, Scotland, before that. The magical garden at Grey Walls, which is so intimately related to the house with stone walls (it was originally called High Walls), shows the unmistakable imprint of Jekyll's ideas about site planning as well as planting, but her role cannot be confirmed due to the loss of any plans that she might have prepared. The house and garden that would come to symbolize the genius of their partnership, however, is Deanery Garden, which was commissioned by Edward Hudson ('Huddy') in 1900. Christopher Hussey called it 'a perfect architectural sonnet', while Lawrence Weaver extolled the way in which house and

garden were welded together into a harmonious whole and commended Jekyll for working with the architect to produce 'effects of singular richness'. The garden indeed is one of richness, restraint, and pleasure. And like Munstead Wood, it was praised for 'having grown out of the landscape rather than [having] been fitted into it.'

Located just outside the village of Sonning, in Berkshire, Deanery Garden was intended as a weekend retreat, where Hudson might spend 'idyllic afternoons beside a Thames backwater.' The 2-acre site captured everyone's imagination with its old brick boundary walls (a remnant possibly from ecclesiastical origins), a river running alongside it, the remains of an orchard planted in the 1860s, and a mass of nettles. On this romantic site, Lutyens created one of his most imaginative early houses and gardens, which Hussey described as 'a single interpenetrating conception – parts roofed over, others open to the sun, with the garden walks leading right into and about

Left: At Deanery Garden the house and garden were in harmony with one another. A terrace connects the garden façade of the house to the lower gardens.

Below: *Convex and concave steps lead from the orchard to the upper courtyard.*

the house, and the windows placed to catch the sparkle of a pool or complete the pattern of a terrace.'

The house, one side of which was tucked up against the external wall along the village street, was built of red brick. One could enter the house through a paved courtyard on the street or go directly into the garden through a small gate. A cloistered walk leads to the fountain court and out into another courtyard with an old pump. A pergola, with alternating round and square brick piers similar to the one at Tigbourne Court, leads out to the gardens, which progress from formal geometric enclosures to the informal wildflower meadow in the apple orchard. Lutyens linked each of the areas with small flights of steps, some square and others semicircular, some concave and others convex.

The centrepiece of the garden plan is a long rill garden, with a central square tank and circular pools at each end, one

recessed under the bridge linking the house with the orchard, and the other, a tank for waterlilies with swags of roses on supports above. It was a playful exercise in geometric games, even to the extent that the stepping stones across the grass alternate between square and diamond shapes. Jekyll's signature herbaceous borders, planted in soft colours with grey foliage, flank the garden with its tiny watercourse running down the centre. The other aspect of the garden scheme is the low buttressed drywalls covered with cluster roses and rock plants. *Rosa* 'The Garland' hanging over the drywalls and rambling roses climbing in the old apple trees help soften the geometric lines of the plan.

Above: *On the upper terrace, a fountain court leads directly to the garden, with the pergola in the distance.*

Right: *A vine-covered pergola runs north and south, with pots of agapanthus at each pier.*

When the house was first featured in *Country Life* in May 1903, the writer called it a house for a man with a hobby. The 'hobby' was roses, but since it's doubtful that Hudson had the time or interest in rose-growing, it may have been another game among close friends. Charles Latham's iconic photographs capture the geometry, detailing, and the lushness of the garden, but the author of the article about it remains unknown, most likely it was E. T. Cook who wrote about Munstead Wood three years earlier. 'The hand of the artist is all the more visible when bloom is most profuse,' the author wrote, 'because the plants have been cunningly arranged to produce grades and shades and harmonies of colours. Here are no wild fantastic discords or glaring effects, but the roses are so arranged as to merge their various shades in a beauty that is grave almost to the point of sadness.' This beautiful house and garden soon passed on to another owner, but Hudson had his eye on a new venture in Northumberland, at Lindisfarne.

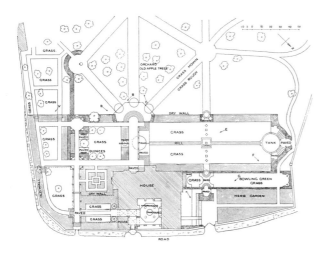

Right: *One of the most distinctive features of the garden plan is the water rill, which runs from a circular pool festooned with roses to a recessed pool under the terrace.*

Marsh Court, Hampshire

Marsh Court stands out as one of Lutyens's most magical houses, taking its inspiration from a grand Tudor manor house, yet built in a highly eclectic mixture of vernacular materials: white chalk, black flint, and red brick. In no other house has he managed to offset a symmetrical plan with such whimsical detailing. The brilliant white façade, with soaring chimney stacks, is dotted with decorative bands of flint, a theme that is carried out in the garden terraces, walls, steps, and ornamental features. Marsh Court (it was originally called Marshcourt) received an unprecedented amount of coverage in *Country Life*, with articles by E. March Phillips, Lawrence Weaver, and Christopher Hussey, the last nearly thirty years after it was first built. The setting is magnificent, on a chalk ridge above the River Test, near Stockbridge, Hampshire. Marsh Court was designed in 1901 for Herbert Johnson, a businessman who admired Lutyens's flair and flamboyance.

He lived here for several decades before it became a preparatory school for boys and girls in 1948, and today it is a private home once again.

The garden scheme consists of a series of terraces hugging the house, with a medley of steps, walls, and balustrades that serve to reinforce the intimacy of house and garden. The centrepiece of the scheme is a sunken pool garden of rectangular shape that functions as an extended wing of the house, while elevated terraces provide additional outdoor spaces. The concept is so beautifully conceived that it is difficult to tell where the house ends and the gardens begin. As Hussey noted, the gardens surround the house 'with that mingling of

Right: *The tile-built pergola incorporates small circular and square tanks filled with waterlilies and other water-loving plants.*

Below: *Lutyens's whimsical façade at Marsh Court features white chalk, red brick, and black flint. The geometric checkerboard theme extends to the garden features.*

conscious design and natural forms that the eye demands for satisfaction.' Where the ground slopes to the river, Lutyens added a lower pergola and twin lily pools that are concealed from view from the upper water garden.

The water garden, which is enclosed by high walls and balustrades, is bisected by a tiny water rill which runs from an elevated cistern down to the rectangular pool. Jekyll's flower borders at the foot of the walls (and also in the other terraces) help deflect the rigid geometry of the overall design. Cubes of clipped boxwood placed along the pool at regular intervals carry out the geometric checkerboard theme estab-

lished throughout the house and garden. Rising from the boxwood cubes, individual lead fountains in the shape of *hippocampi* (sea horses) spout water from their muzzles. These enchanting creatures were designed by Julia Chance, the sculptor-owner of Orchards. 'Water takes its highest place in garden architecture when it determines the complete design of an enclosed space, such as the pool garden at Marsh Court devised by Mr Lutyens,' wrote Jekyll. Marsh Court remains one of the most delightful of all the water gardens designed by Lutyens and Jekyll and served as a prototype for others that followed.

Above: *The water garden is enclosed by high walls with geometric steps leading down to the rectangular tank filled with waterlilies.*

Left: *The lily pool in the sunken terrace is ornamented with cubes of boxwood and lead fountains in the shape of seahorses spouting water.*

Millmead, Surrey

Lutyens continued to experiment with the ideal small manor house, and one of his best was Little Thakeham in Storrington, Sussex. His client, E. M. Blackburn, was an ardent gardener himself, which may explain why Jekyll was not involved in the commission. At Little Thakeham, Lutyens provided the garden framework based on ideas used in other projects, including a rose garden, lily pool, and generous lawn with an elevated pergola. The result was quite pleasant, but lacked the inventiveness and sophisticated planting component that Jekyll contributed to all their collaborations. However, in 1905 Lutyens and Jekyll put their heads together to create the best small house they could, one that would be noteworthy for its architectural merit, convenience, and comfort, as described in *Gardens for Small Country Houses*.

It was Jekyll who spotted a derelict plot of land in Bramley village, not far from Munstead Wood, and decided to build a new house and garden on what she called the 'sordid half-acre' site. The long narrow plot (80 feet by 400 feet), which sloped down to a rushing millstream, provided the name for the new house, Millmead. Located on Snowdenham Lane, where some old cottages had been pulled down, the site offered interesting challenges. It was Jekyll's idea to buy the

land and commission Lutyens to build a house that was 'reminiscent of some of the small houses of good type built in England under Dutch influence in the early years of the eighteenth century.' The small, elegant house was built of Bargate stone with a tile roof, but the details were classical rather than Lutyens's former Surrey style. Tipping sniffed that the modest house was 'rather over-windowed', but on the whole he quite approved and in fact praised Lutyens for 'showing us how perfect a thing a little country house on a tiny plot of ground can be made [and] transformed into an earthly paradise.'

Lutyens provided the essential enclosure by adding a tile-coped wall along the street front and down the two long sides of the property that lead to the stream below. Jekyll's delightful garden was simple in concept, consisting of three long terraces, each with a different character. For a small plot of only $\frac{1}{2}$ acre, there were many excesses, including three small summerhouses that Lutyens managed to squeeze in, as well as Jekyll's numerous, intensively planted borders. For a house and garden built on speculation, it was a fantasy to expect the owner to maintain such a confection and today only the bare outlines of the garden remain in place. As was

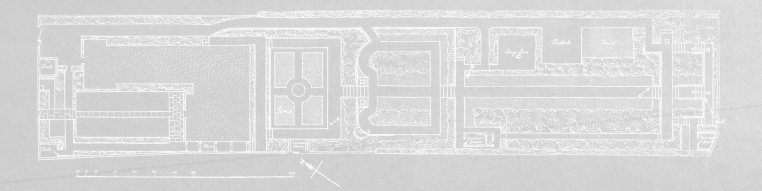

Left: *The summerhouse at Millmead is one of several on the small site. A tile-coped wall provides essential enclosure to the garden.*

Below: *Steps to the lower level and a sundial. Jekyll's planting scheme includes veronica, London Pride, dianthus, mullein, and sweet William.*

Hestercombe Gardens, Somerset

Hestercombe Gardens in Somerset is one of Lutyens and Jekyll's grandest and most sophisticated projects and one that gave wider recognition to both designers. In 1908, when the garden was newly completed, Avray Tipping marvelled at the high level of craftsmanship and the ingenuity shown in melding formality with nature, while Lawrence Weaver in 1913 declared that Lutyens had brought to the design 'invention and ingenuity, imagination and learning.' In 1927, Christopher Hussey remarked that twenty years earlier 'this garden seemed essentially an architect's garden – rather hard and cold. Now an impressionist painter would be proud to own such colour and lightness.' Jekyll's name is absent from all these articles, yet in 1950 Hussey paid tribute to her in *The Life of Sir Edwin Lutyens*: 'The Hestercombe gardens represent the peak of the collaboration with Miss Jekyll, and

[Lutyens's] first application of her genius to classical garden design on a grand scale.'

Lutyens received the commission in 1903 from the Hon. E. W. B. Portman, who undoubtedly selected him based on his popularity among the fashionable set, but the commission was unusual because it entailed a garden only and not a new house. Lutyens made up for this by adding several significant new structures, including an elegant classical orangery. In addition, there was an historically important eighteenth-century landscape garden already in place, and rather than obliterating the earlier landscape, he created visual links to it

Above: *The great plat at Hestercombe Gardens with distant views to the Vale of Taunton.*

Right: *The east rill is part of an elaborate water garden at Hestercombe, which starts under the house terrace and flows into holding tanks.*

from the new garden. The original garden had been created around 1770 by Copplestone Warre Bampfylde, a well-known painter, in the prevailing landscape style, with follies, temples, ponds, cascades, and wonderful vistas.

The site in the Quantock Hills overlooking the Vale of Taunton in Somerset was breathtaking, but the original eighteenth-century house had been badly remodelled during the Victorian era by Portman's grandfather, who also added a new terrace at the same time. Lutyens chose to turn his back on the Victorian ensemble and create a new, classically-inspired formal garden that could be admired from the terrace. He took advantage of the sloping ground below the house to create a series of terraces, the centrepiece of which was a large, flat parterre (a sunken plat) bounded by a long pergola that framed the views to the hills beyond. The plat, which was 125 feet square, was flanked by two elevated water terraces each 140 feet long. On the west side, the water terrace was extended to create a rectangular rose garden with

a sheltered alcove that was adjacent to the original terrace.
On the east side he created a rotunda, with high circular stone
walls and planted with fragrant wintersweet.

The formality of the plan was offset by Lutyens's imaginative use of materials, mostly rough-split local stone in a
warm grey tone, while in other areas that required more
architectural definition he used a yellow Ham stone. The
geometric theme was carried out in his signature steps, both
square and round, inspired to some degree by those at
Owlpen Manor in Gloucestershire. The pergola which frames
the view out consists of alternating square and round piers.
Ovoid openings in the enclosure walls, similar to the ancient
loopholes he saw at Great Tangley Manor with Jekyll in the
1890s, provide glimpses to the pasture beyond.

Jekyll used the soft grey colour of the stone as her planting
inspiration. The fragrant grey walk on a level just below the
Victorian terrace was flanked by double borders composed of
grey and silver foliage with tones of blue, purple, and white
for the flowers. In the plat and the side borders, the plantings

The water terrace, with stone-edged paths and a stone water channel, runs perpendicular to a long pergola with a break for enjoying the view.

(left above): *view from the rotunda to the plat;* (left below): *the rotunda and pool;*
(this page above): *spouting masque and pool which is part of the water system;*
(below): *the great plat with central sundial and triangular-shaped beds.*

Overleaf: *The pergola, built of rough-split local stone, is smothered in climbing vines; at the end of the walk, there is a loophole opening in the wall.*

were more boldly conceived and brilliantly coloured. The triangular-shaped beds in the great plat, which were formed by the two long diagonal grass walks converging in a central sundial, were filled with a striking combination of cannas, gladioli, delphiniums, and *Lilium candidum*, and edged with *Bergenia cordifolia*. The plantings were later replaced by a more pleasing composition of roses, peonies, and delphiniums. The borders along the elevated water rills were planted in cool tones on the west side and warmer tones on the east side. Almost all of the original plants at Hestercombe came from the nursery at Munstead Wood.

One of the glorious aspects of Hestercombe is the elaborate water system, where water drips from a lion's masque into a recessed circular pool, then runs down the parallel rills and collects in rectangular tanks adjacent to the pergola. The pergola is discontinuous in front of these tanks in order to create a *claire voyée* to the distant landscape. 'The planted rill may be considered the invention of Sir Edwin Lutyens,' Jekyll wrote in *Wall and Water Gardens*. ' The wide paved ledges make pleasant walking ways; at even intervals they turn, after the manner of the gathered ribbon strapwork of ancient needlework, and enclose circular tanklets, giving the opportunity of a distinct punctuation with important plants.' Jekyll planted the rills with arum lily, iris, water plantain, and forget-me-nots. The water theme was also carried out in the rose garden, where there is a smaller rill, and in a circular mirror pool in the rotunda that reflects the clouds in the sky.

After the garden was constructed and planted, Lutyens was asked to extend the garden further in 1906. This is when he

Above: *Lutyens's rotunda, built with yellow Ham stone and rough shale, was intended as a winter garden.*

Left: *A striking combination of cannas, gladioli, and* Bergenia cordifolia *in the plat beds. The wide grass walks are edged with local stone.*

designed the orangery on the eastern section of land beyond the rotunda and overlooking the lawns that were once part of Bampfylde's parkland. This magnificent William and Mary-style building, constructed from shale and handsomely dressed with Ham stone, was reached by a flight of steps that leads down to the rotunda. The orangery terrace repeated the design forms of the plat. At the same time Lutyens also designed an elevated 'Dutch' garden (although there was no traditional topiary) reached via a flight of steps up from the orangery. The site had formerly been the rubbish tip and included an old mill building at the far end. Jekyll designed a small parterre garden based on grey foliage and ornamented with antique Italian terracotta urns in each of the beds. Each

Above: Lutyens's magnificent orangery overlooks the original eighteenth-century lawn.

Left: Jekyll's fragrant grey walk, below the house terrace, is filled with striking combinations of blue, purple, and white flowers and grey foliage.

Overleaf: The elevated 'Dutch' garden, up a flight of steps from the orangery, is a small parterre with predominantly grey foliage and Italian terracotta urns in each bed.

bed was planted with China roses, yuccas, lavender, nepeta, and 'that rather dull plant, the grey-leaved Stachys,' to quote Tipping. Overall, Tipping found the Dutch garden 'rather too much an architect's garden and too little a gardener's garden.' Lutyens played the final trick in this garden, where a door opens out onto the main vista of the eighteenth-century garden.

Portman only enjoyed his garden for a few years and after his death in 1911, his wife continued to live at Hestercombe until 1953, at which time it was turned over to the Somerset County Council. After years of decline, the formal gardens were restored in 1973 following the discovery of a set of Jekyll's planting plans in the garden shed. In more recent years the landscape garden has also been fully restored. This large and complex garden remains one of the most inspirational of all the Lutyens and Jekyll collaborations, drawing thousands of visitors from around the world every year who come to admire the architectural detailing and the outstanding plantings.

Folly Farm, Berkshire

If Hestercombe was their grandest garden, Folly Farm represents Lutyens and Jekyll's most ingenious collaboration. Lanning Roper, the renowned American landscape architect who later advised on the gardens, credited Lutyens for his ingenuity and creative genius as a landscape architect and Jekyll for her sensitivity and imagination as a gardener. The project is unusual in several respects, the first being that Lutyens and Jekyll designed the gardens twice, once for the initial client and then for the subsequent owner in a completely different mood. Another remarkable aspect is that the designers' collaborative efforts are clearly visible on the original working plans that passed back and forth between the two. They are filled with queries, such as 'steps up to the croquet lawn?', and replies ('no'), which confirm Jekyll's role as a designer rather than a mere gardening consultant. Neither Weaver, nor Hussey, nor Tipping breathed Jekyll's name in their respective reviews, instead directing all their praise to Lutyens.

In 1906, H. H. Cochrane, a wealthy businessman, asked Lutyens to design an addition to an old farmhouse and former dairy farm in Sulhamstead, near Reading. The original cottage and barns were located on a busy village street, so Lutyens created several courtyard enclosures to link these old

Lutyens's loggia and square lily tank, one of several water features at Folly Farm, overlooks Jekyll's grand flower parterre.

buildings with the new addition, an enchanting William and Mary-inspired house built of silver-coloured bricks and dressed with bright red brick trim. The new entrance court, which one entered through an emerald green gate from the street, was a formal green parterre planted with Jekyll's restrained palette of small shrubs and climbers, such as climbing roses, clematis, and jasmine. A paved path led through a brick-capped archway to the adjacent barn court, with borders of roses, dianthus, lavender, and other cottage-style plants in soft tones and edged with bergenia and lambs' ears. An Italian oil jar on a pedestal marked the turning of the path towards the original farmhouse. The narrow brick path within the paved walk was laid in a herringbone pattern that was repeated throughout the garden. The parterre in front of the main façade was a simple croquet lawn and close by, a

rhododendron walk. Early photographs show a dianthus-lined grass walk backed by a rose-covered latticework fence enclosing the lawn on the west side. The gardens were pleasant, but unremarkable.

In 1912, at the request of the new owner, Zachary Merton, these gardens were transformed into one of the most remarkable designs of the early twentieth century. Each new area and earlier portions that were reworked were defined with long yew hedges, which created a series of 'rooms', not unlike those at Hidcote and later at Sissinghurst. In all, there were seven individual enclosures not counting a large, walled kitchen garden. Lutyens added a new wing to the earlier addition so that the Mertons could have more guest rooms and a sizable dining room, but instead of simply extending the symmetrical 1906 wing, Lutyens took his

inspiration from traditional barn buildings with their low, swooping rooflines in order to accommodate the slope of the ground to the west. The new wing, which more than doubled the size of the earlier addition, provided a rather startling contrast with the staid building and one of his most distinctive architectural essays.

A new courtyard between the buildings was transformed into a buttressed loggia hugging a square lily tank, one of three new water features to be added. The former grass walk along the edge of the 1906 building was expanded to become an elaborate parterre garden with billowing flowers in shades of blue and purple. This new garden offset the distinctive gabled front of the new extension. Herringbone brick paths divided the space into four major quadrants and numerous flower beds.

But the improvements didn't stop there. One of the most distinctive design features of the 1912 scheme is the long canal that replaced the earlier croquet lawn. It was based on Dutch-inspired canal gardens that were popular in England in the late seventeenth century, such as the one at Westbury Court in Gloucestershire. It was definitely a more serene solution than the overly detailed sunken water garden at Marsh Court and was flanked by luxuriant borders along the edges. The long expanse of water, which acted as a mirror for Lutyens's addition, was separated from the adjacent parterre garden by a long yew hedge, one of several that enclose each of the major areas and prevent one from seeing across from one area to the next.

Above: *A brick-capped archway leads to the barn court with an Italian oil jar on a pedestal. The plantings in the court are in soft tones and edged with bergenia and lambs' ears.*

Left: *The elaborate parterre garden in front of the loggia wing has borders of blue and purple flowers flanked by a herringbone-patterned brick walk.*

There was also a long yew walk leading out from the western end of the addition as well as a lime tree walk, both of which reinforced the axial geometry of the garden. The most elaborate of the new areas is the unusual sunken garden to the west of the parterre garden. A square garden, it is enclosed on all sides by high, thick hedges and sits in the lowest part of the ground. Lutyens's signature circular steps at each of the four corners descend to the water parterre, with a central octagonal pool and island beds originally filled with heathers, but later replaced with beds of fragrant lavender. It was a magical, secret garden from which to catch glimpses of the dormers and chimneys of the new addition. As in most of the areas of the gardens, Jekyll kept her plantings fairly simple so as to not disturb the dominant architecture.

Lutyens's client was unlucky in his short enjoyment of the grand gardens, and after Merton's death in 1915, his widow, who was a great friend of Lady Emily Lutyens, lent the family the house for the summer. This was perhaps the only time that Lutyens had the opportunity to live in one of his own houses. In the 1920s, Folly Farm was owned by Arthur Gilbey and from 1951 onwards by the Astor family, both of whom made some changes to the gardens. In 1971, the Astors called in Lanning Roper for advice on simplifying the garden.

Working with the old *Country Life* photographs, he retained the remarkable structure of the gardens, but refreshed the plantings in several areas. In the sunken rose garden, for example, he replaced the languishing lavender with *Senecio greyi*, and added modern, more carefree roses. He eliminated the borders along the canal and cleared out the waterlilies to give the garden a sleek contemporary look. He also grassed-over the dense plantings in the parterre, while injecting better-performing perennials into the outer borders. Roper, an occasional writer for *Country Life* and a great admirer of Jekyll, remarked that Folly Farm was a garden of vistas, each area distinct in its personality, yet linked to the next. Folly Farm is still privately owned and remains an excellent example of the legendary design principles of both Lutyens and Jekyll.

Above: *Lutyens's distinctive circular steps in each of the four corners of the sunken water parterre.*

Right: *The long canal garden* (above) *was originally flanked with double borders, but they were later removed* (below) *when the garden was simplified.*

Lindisfarne Castle, Northumberland

In addition to working with Lutyens on some of the most memorable houses built during the Edwardian era, Jekyll also advised on gardens for three castles, including Castle Drogo, Devon, a granite folly built for Julius Drewe in 1915. While the building was underway, Lutyens had asked Jekyll to provide plans for informal plantings along the modest entrance drive. But her scheme for terraces below the castle was rejected by the client and the formal gardens were largely the work of George Dillistone in the 1920s. Lutyens may not have always had his way with his clients, but his design ingenuity at Castle Drogo was clearly the result of his prior experience in renovating two dilapidated castles each with very different gardens, and both on remote islands.

Lindisfarne Castle, perched on a tidal island three miles out from Berwick-upon-Tweed in Northumberland, would become one of Lutyens's most renowned commissions, and along with Castle Drogo, the only property by the architect to be owned by the National Trust. His client was Edward Hudson, who had been searching for another holiday retreat

ever since relinquishing Deanery Garden. He contacted Lutyens early in 1902 to say he had found an abandoned Tudor castle on Holy Island, near the former Benedictine priory made famous by the Lindisfarne Gospels. The uninhabited castle literally grew out from the rock, but Hudson could see the possibilities. It proved an impractical folly, since Hudson spent most of his time in London, but he and Lutyens had a wonderful time fixing it up before he eventually sold it in 1920. The interiors were austere and inhospitable according to guests (who included Lady Emily Lutyens and Queen Mary), but for Lutyens it was an exercise in archaeological accuracy. The country house connoisseur James Lees-Milne remarked that it was 'a charming little castle, all stone steps and passageways with low vaulted ceilings.'

In May 1906, Jekyll accompanied Lutyens across the sandy causeway in order to discuss possibilities for a garden with Hudson. Hudson dreamed of an elaborate water garden in the valley surrounding the castle and wanted to turn the old walled garden across the field into a tennis court. As work

progressed on the castle and the budget escalated, Hudson realized that the best thing to do was to revive the old walled garden and forget about making an elaborate new garden. In 1911, Jekyll drew up two planting plans for the walled garden, but not before Lutyens rebuilt two of the walls and readjusted the path grid so that the walled enclosure was visually aligned from the windows in the upper battery of the castle. Jekyll took as her inspiration the wildflowers growing in the rocks and in the local village. One plan was for the initial year and composed primarily of vegetable and annuals, while the second one was for a more permanent planting of perennials, annuals, shrubs, and roses, with only a single border assigned to vegetables.

The charming garden, which is roughly 75 feet square (but really an irregular trapezoid), was broken into long borders along the sides and five, small island beds in the centre. The western border is filled with hybrid tea and Bourbon roses, the northern with showy perennials (hollyhocks, sunflowers,

Japanese anemones, and gladioli), and the eastern border was devoted to fruits and vegetables. The island beds contained grey-foliage plants, including hundreds of *Stachys byzantina*, which were mixed with campanulas, sweet peas, centaureas, delphiniums, and other blue and white flowers. The effect was pure Jekyll, from the grey foliage to the cool and warm flower tones to set off the warm grey of the local stone used in the walls and in the paving.

The garden ran into problems right from the start, the major one being the lack of a source for water – the original well had been mistakenly paved over during construction, plus many of the plants grown in the warmer soil at Munstead Wood failed to survive the windy and salty Northumberland climate. Today this tiny little garden, which has recently been restored, is ablaze with many of Jekyll's favourite plants.

The tiny walled garden at Lindisfarne Castle is located some distance from the castle and ablaze with sea-loving plants.

climate, and over the years most of the plantings were simplified or abolished.

In the north court between the new service wing and the old dwelling Lutyens rescued the existing pillars from an old cowshed to create a pergola along one side. Jekyll's planting suggestions include her tried-and-true selection of *Clematis montana*, roses, and jasmine as luxuriant cover for the piers, as well as clusters of astilbes, fuchsias, delphiniums, and bold groups of acanthus in the traditional long border. For the borders surrounding the grass court and paving in the east court, she suggested lilies, peonies, and hydrangeas with grey foliage plants, such as santolinas and rosemary. The west entrance court consisted of two long panels of grass and paved path bisected by a small iris rill and recessed pool similar to the one at Deanery Garden. Writing in 1913, Lawrence Weaver remarked that the garden areas were not yet fully mature, but they were pleasantly laid out in a sympathetic way, 'the scheme of plantings devised by Miss Jekyll with her usual skill.' But in reality these labour-intensive borders for all their beauty could be enjoyed for only two months of the year. What seemed to impress visitors more than the designed areas was the riot of bloom all over the island. 'Lambay is an island of flowers', wrote Weaver. Grass, bracken, heath, rush, stonecrop, *Scilla verna*, sea pinks, and yellow lichen bloom and, as all over Ireland, fuchsias flourish everywhere, even today.

Above: *The pillars from an old cowshed were transformed into a pergola in the north court.* Clematis montana, *roses, and jasmine covered the piers.*

Right: *The romantic setting for Lambay, where Lutyens transformed old buildings and designed new ones in the old style.*

Gledstone Hall, Yorkshire

If Lambay was a welcoming retreat, Gledstone Hall in Yorkshire was cold and austere by contrast. After a hiatus of nearly fifteen years, while Lutyens was engaged in New Delhi and elsewhere, and Jekyll was working on numerous other projects, the partners came together again for an awe-inspiring finale to the country house garden. According to Christopher Hussey, there was no better example of their collaboration because it combined architectural form with impressionistic planting.

The client was Sir Amos Nelson, whom Lutyens had met on a voyage out to India. Sir Amos bought the property near Skipton in North Yorkshire in 1923 with the intention of enlarging an old Georgian hall by John Carr of York. But on second thoughts, the prospect from the high point of the site was so engaging that he asked for a new house and had the old hall demolished several years later. Lutyens built a Palladian-style house to emulate the earlier hall, but the local

grey sandstone with which it was built was as cold as the climate. Lutyens took advantage of the south-sloping site by placing the house on the precipice and laying out the formal gardens below. As was the case at Deanery Garden, Marsh Court, and other earlier houses, there was no hint of the grand garden at the entrance, but the geometry of the plain circular forecourt is a theme throughout the garden.

At the time of the commission Lutyens was in his mid-fifties and Jekyll had just turned eighty-two. She was nearly blind, but nonetheless she turned out dozens of planting plans for the elaborate gardens. She did not visit the site, but asked for soil samples and enquired about the colour of the stone before selecting her plants. Working primarily from memory,

Above: *The west terrace, with wide walkways and deep herbaceous borders, harked back to earlier Jekyll-Lutyens collaborations, such as Hestercombe Gardens in 1906.*

Right: *Jekyll's tried-and-true foliage plantings in the loggia parterre at Gledstone Hall.*

she designed border after border using her old favourites, such as *Stachys lanata*, bergenias, monardas, aruncus, spireas, and a host of labour-intensive annuals and perennials, most of which came by rail from the Munstead Wood nursery. The initial plant list was for over seven hundred different types of plants. A rare surviving invoice she submitted in 1928 for a shipment of plants totalled £93 and her design fee was 105 guineas. The previous year she had complained to Lutyens's office, 'Nothing yet from Sir Amos Nelson, but the near prospect of £105 warms the cockles of the depleted exchequer!'

The grand garden scheme revisited all the familiar elements from earlier projects, such as a long canal (nearly 200 feet long) with a recessed pool, flanking terraces, and an elevated pergola to frame the vista in the distance (the planned extension of the garden beyond the pergola was never built). Unique to the project was an elevated circular pool at the far end of the canal where the ground drops off steeply. As at Folly Farm, the water level came just to the rim so that the building façade could be admirably reflected. The terraces flanking the long pool align with the twin porticoes of the house. Loggias from the projecting wings of the house have their own rose-filled parterres and are paved with slate tiles arranged in patterns. In 1935, a few years after Jekyll's death, Hussey wrote that 'the effect is lovely, toning in with the big soft *pouffes* of lavender and santolina and mahonia lying between alternate columns.' The pillars are entwined with wisteria. On the descent to the pool, Jekyll used strong colours and dramatic foliage, such as *Bergenia cordifolia* (a favourite at Hestercombe), *Acanthus mollis*, Rodgersia, and red-hot pokers.

In its glory, the gardens harked back to an earlier era and as Hussey remarked: 'it is expensive to build an architectural garden of the kind that preserves a constant beauty not only through the seasons and the years, but through the centuries.' The making of such gardens was becoming *passé* in the mid-1920s and as the maintenance lapsed, the gardens began to disappear. Jekyll quickly discovered that many of the Surrey-grown plants she specified simply did not flourish in Yorkshire and substitutes had to be brought in. The gardens slipped into obscurity during successive ownerships and more recently, when Gledstone was a nursing facility for the elderly, the gardens suffered enormously. The present owner, an artist, hopes to revive this once-grand house and garden.

The long canal, which reflects the garden façade, stretches nearly 200 feet from the recessed pool under the terrace to the elevated pool adjacent to the pergola.

use of primulas throughout, as well as the irises and roses that
had been recommended by Jekyll, but in the end failed to
mention her name. Not one to credit herself for anything, she
would have joined in the praise for Lutyens.

Above: *The outstanding naturalistic gardens at Plumpton Place include some of
Jekyll's recommendations for roses and irises.*

Left: *Steps on the moated island, with luxuriant ornamental trees, shrubs, and
climbers.*

Right: *Jekyll's planting plans for the double borders for the main house were among
her last designs.*

Colour in the Flower Garden

....

*"To plant
and maintain a
flower-border,
with a good
scheme for colour,
is by no means
the easy thing
that is commonly
supposed."*

....

*Colour-themed borders at The Manor House at
Upton Grey, Hampshire.*

In addition to her fabled work with Lutyens, Jekyll designed numerous gardens on her own or in collaboration with nearly fifty other architects, but these gardens rarely appeared in the pages of *Country Life*. Sometimes the gardens were overlooked in articles about the architects' houses; in other instances, the architects with whom she collaborated were allied with *The Studio* magazine, whose market was middle-class art-lovers, rather than with *Country Life*, which appealed to the leisured upper-class sporting set.

Country Life presented a somewhat unbalanced view of current architecture and garden design, paying scant tribute to Thomas Mawson, for example, who was one of the era's most prolific garden architects. The architects with whom Jekyll was associated ranged from such national figures as Robert Lorimer, M. H. Baillie Scott, and Herbert Baker to lesser-known names, like L. Rome Guthrie, Thackeray Turner, Harold Falkner, and Walter Brierley. All were in one way or the other influenced by the Arts and Crafts movement, which honoured the use of local materials, expert craftsmanship, and had a reverence for regional design traditions. This movement extended to the art of garden design, for which Jekyll was the chief proponent.

There is little doubt that Jekyll's best gardens are those for which an architect provided a basic layout, which she used as a starting point for her incomparable flower borders. These were based on her tried-and-true theories which she had been perfecting for decades and which she explained in some detail in her book *Colour in the Flower Garden* (1908). Often working from memory, she would execute her designs rapidly and with ease, provided she had soil samples, chips of local stone, and photographs showing the topography. In some cases, when she worked outside of her familiar home territory, she ran afoul of the climate and growing conditions that were inhospitable to her Surrey-grown plants. In general, though, her border designs were based on plantings of hardy perennials in colours and textures that suited the individual situations.

The rose-laden pergola at The Manor House, Upton Grey, connects the house with the steps leading down to the lower gardens.

While her working relationships with architects were always cordial, none was as harmonious and successful as that with Lutyens, whom she took as her standard. She once described the difference between working with Lutyens and the Scottish architect Robert Lorimer as that between quicksilver and suet. On the other hand, few architects had the sureness of touch or fundamental understanding of landscape that Lutyens had. Lorimer, who had many good things to say about Munstead Wood when it was under construction, sought Jekyll's advice on two early Surrey houses, Whinfold for Lionel Benson in 1897 and High Barn for the Hon. Stuart Pleydell-Bouverie in 1901, as well as three later projects. Lorimer's Scottish houses and gardens were championed by *Country Life*, starting with his youthful renovations in 1891 of Earlshall Castle, but his projects with Jekyll were overlooked. Jekyll was a great admirer of Lorimer and included examples of his garden architecture in *Garden Ornament* (1918). Another architect with whom she had sympathy was Oliver Hill, a young follower of Lutyens whose work was featured in *Country Life*. One architect with whom she failed to get on with was Sidney Barnsley. At Combend Manor in Gloucestershire in 1925, they sparred over details and his replies to her detailed queries and suggestions left something to be desired.

She worked with M. H. Baillie Scott on several commissions, but at East Runton Hall near the windswept seacoast of North Norfolk, the client rejected her schemes for a rose garden and a fragrant parterre garden. Whatever reservations Jekyll had about working with difficult clients or architects, she must have enjoyed collaborating with architects who were in sympathy with the finer points of garden design.

The Manor House, Upton Grey, Hampshire

From the early 1900s on, Jekyll worked on four or five commissions a year for private clients, many of whom came from her circle of family friends, neighbours, and artists. She especially liked working for clients who were knowledgeable about horticulture and appreciated gardens, whether they lived near Munstead or farther afield, such as the Marchioness of Londonderry in Ireland. Due to the lack of correspondence relating to her commissions, it is often difficult to determine how some of her clients approached her. Her name was well known through her books and her association with *Country Life*, so it is likely that some requests were forwarded by the magazine.

Above: *The low drystone walls are planted with grey-foliage wall plants anchored by two* Buxus sempervirens *flanking the steps.*

Left: *Clusters of* Lilium regale *in a raised stone bed in the rose parterre. The trapezoidal borders in the parterre are planted with roses, lilies, and peonies and edged with lambs' ears.*

Overleaf: *Lush double herbaceous borders arranged in cool and warm tones are backed by a clipped hedge. The orchard is in the distance.*

One case in point is a splendid garden, one of the few extant ones from this period, in which the circumstances of the commission are somewhat cloudy. In 1908, when she was sixty-five, Jekyll received a commission from a Mr Best for a garden at the old manor house at Upton Grey in Hampshire. Best was the tenant of the manor house which was actually owned by Charles Holme, a well-known textile merchant and arts collector, who was also the founder and editor of *The Studio*. After Holme left William Morris's Red House in Bexleyheath in 1902, he began buying up most of the village of Upton Grey. Oddly he lived at Upton Grey House, rather than the manor house, but was nonetheless responsible for hiring Ernest Newton, an important Arts and Crafts architect, to transform the old Tudor farmhouse into a comfortable Edwardian retreat. Perhaps, like Hudson, he envisioned a life in the country that never quite materialized. Newton's renovations were completed by 1907 and shortly thereafter Jekyll was consulted about the garden, one of her most successful projects to date.

As was usually the case, the architects provided a set of plans for use in designing the garden scheme. The site (which she never visited) was modest, just under 5 acres, on sloping ground behind the house. For the formal gardens at the back of the house, Jekyll immediately eliminated the grass banks installed by Holme and broke the ground into several terraces bounded by low drystone walls, just as she had done at Millmead a couple of years earlier. The scheme was simple, an upper terrace with a pergola connecting the house to the first set of steps down to the formal rose parterre, beyond which were two more areas: a long bowling green, and a tennis lawn below that. Opposite the front forecourt is a large wild garden that abuts the local twelfth-century church. Today, the property is surrounded by a nuttery and a walled orchard, as well as a new Jekyll-style kitchen garden with double herbaceous borders. The present owners bought the derelict property in 1984 and set to work bringing the house and garden back to its original beauty. In so doing they have created one of the most authentic of all the Jekyll restorations by closely following the original planting plans and searching out the best available plants.

The configuration of the rectangular rose lawn was similar to others she had designed elsewhere, except for two raised beds for floral display built of the same local Bargate stone as the walls. Her original planting plans indicate clumps of cannas and lilies in pots (similar to the arrangement in the water garden at Munstead Wood). The four trapezoidal borders surrounding each stone bed were planted with roses,

Paved and grass walkways at Upton flank deep borders filled with some of Jekyll's favourite plants.

Overleaf: *Brilliant red poppies punctuate the Jekyll-esque drifts of yellow, white, mauve, and blue flowers.*

148

lilies, and peonies and edged with lambs' ears, a tried-and-true favourite. The main event for Jekyll was the luscious composition of grey-themed wall plants, such as rosemary, lavender, cerastium, iris, acanthus, hostas, and santolina. The upper borders were filled with daylilies, dianthus, iris, anemones, alyssum, poppies, and penstemon. The effect again was similar to that at Millmead. The pergola connecting the house with the rose lawn was smothered with several different old-fashioned climbing roses ('Jersey Beauty', 'Reine Olga de Wurtemberg', 'Blush' and 'Dundee' ramblers, and Jekyll's favourite, 'The Garland'). The double borders in the kitchen garden are arranged in 'cool' and 'warm' tones that emulate Jekyll's long border at Munstead Wood. A number of the original plants came from Jekyll's nursery at Munstead Wood.

The wild garden, one of the few extant examples from all of Jekyll's commissions, is one of the most significant areas at Upton Grey. Irregular mown paths meander from the entrance to a pond, all planted naturalistically with clumps of walnuts, quince, bamboo, hollies, yew, and many ornamental shrubs. In the spring it is carpeted with drifts of daffodils, some of which are Jekyll's original bulbs. Snowdrops, primroses, oxlips, cowslips, and others are also survivors from an earlier era. The garden at Upton Grey has everything that Jekyll treasured in a garden: a simple plan with borders filled with favourite flowers, a generous amount of green lawn, and an enchanting wild garden. The play between formality and informality has been achieved in the best possible way.

Above: *The recently refurbished original glasshouse in the kitchen garden is edged with towering hollyhocks.*

Left: *In the wild garden, mown paths meander down to the pond. The garden is planted with rambling roses, as well as wildflowers and ornamental trees and shrubs.*

Bishopsbarns, York

Jekyll had a sympathetic relationship with Walter Brierley, a talented architect from York, whose houses have been somewhat overshadowed by those by Lutyens. Brierley was a master of detail and known for his Arts and Crafts Tudor-style houses, notably his home, Bishopsbarns in St. George's Place, York. Bishopsbarns was not exactly a country house because of its location in a suburb of York, but Brierley's ingenious placing of the house on the site gives it the quality of a country house rather than a suburban one. The quaintly gabled house, built of rich red brick, has no front garden to speak of since the entrance is so close to the street. Instead the small back garden was well planned to incorporate a tennis court, pergola, bowling green, and grass terraces, all enclosed with a dense hedge of cypress and other trees and shrubs to help screen the neighbouring houses.

Lawrence Weaver's glowing appraisal of the garden in *Small Country Houses of To-Day* in 1910 stated: 'For the garden at Bishopsbarns there can be nothing but praise. For though it is small the best use has been made of the available space, and its planting was devised by Miss Jekyll.' The colour schemes were worked out in consummate detail.

'Sitting in the loggia, one sees across the warm brick paving of the path the grey of stachys receding through the light turquoise of Japanese iris and the powerful blues of delphinium to the backing of deep green in the trim yew hedge.' Jekyll's signature flower borders, which Weaver admired from the loggia, flank a long bowling green, and masses of lupins make a fine play against the house. She prepared a detailed garden plan based on a plan provided by Brierley in 1905, and sent him lists of cutting flowers and rambling roses for the pergola. She also provided plans for two other Brierley houses, Bishopthorpe Paddock and Dyke Nook Lodge in 1907.

Above: *From the loggia of Bishopsbarns, Walter Brierley's home in York, one could admire Jekyll's signature flower borders and the bowling green.*

Right: *Masses of lupins against the gabled house are part of Jekyll's colour scheme.*

Vann, Surrey

Not surprisingly Jekyll designed or advised on a number of gardens in her own area, which were often of modest size and executed for friends and neighbours. They lack the characteristic complex layouts of those on which she collaborated with Lutyens and other architects, and instead have more informal plantings. For these clients Jekyll would draw up lists of plants that she could supply from her nursery rather than provide full sets of planting plans. One case in point is the remarkable woodland stream garden at Vann, secluded deep in the countryside only a few miles from Munstead Wood. It is probably her best surviving water garden and still has

many plants that have naturalized from those that were originally supplied.

In 1907, W. D. Caröe leased an old Surrey farmhouse with origins in the sixteenth-century as a home in the country. An architect, Caröe ended up doubling the size of the original building over the next few years and created a rambling Arts and Crafts complex. When he began his renovations, there was little left of the original garden except some old fruit trees and a small cottage garden at the entrance to the original house. He proceeded to lay out various garden areas hugging the buildings, including a superb pergola built of rough masonry that nicely complemented the old tile-hung house with distinctive weather-boarding.

In 1911, Caröe and his wife consulted Jekyll about a new garden in the stream valley below the house, where he had created several small pools connected with informal winding

Above: W. D. Caröe's pergola built of rough masonry perfectly complements the old tile-hung house.

Left: The cottage garden at the entrance to the original house at Vann.

stone paths and bridges. By January 1912, Jekyll had drawn up a list of over 1,500 plants, which she could supply from Munstead Wood. Her recommendations included hellebores, iris, ferns, hostas, marsh marigolds, Solomon's seal, bog myrtle, fritillarias, and other plants that would happily thrive in a shady wet area. Jekyll's vision for this subtle water garden drew on her skills in integrating a naturalistic garden into a modest landscape with some formal elements, just as she had accomplished so well at Munstead Wood. Over the years the various garden areas were enlarged and Jekyll's plants continued to thrive in the water garden. The present generation of Caröes has ably transformed this comfortable compound into a major garden, and all the while Jekyll's original plants continue to thrive.

Above: *The naturalistic water garden ties in perfectly with the more formal areas around the house.*

Left: *Jekyll supplied many plants for the woodland stream garden at Vann, including iris, ferns, hostas, and marsh marigolds, which continue to thrive today.*

Highmount, Surrey

In contrast to the intimacy and charm of Vann, Jekyll revealed another side of her talents in an extensive, brand-new suburban garden, just outside Guildford. Highmount, as the name implies, stands on a chalk ridge above the town, with expansive views over the countryside. The garden had already been laid out to a certain degree, presumably by the architect, Douglas G. Round, when Jekyll was brought in around 1909. Already in place were a tennis lawn, croquet lawn, and bowling green, but Jekyll thought the steeply sloping site below the house offered opportunities for creating a series of terraces instead of the present grassy slopes with undistinguished plantings. Her ideas entailed 'a serious amount of moving of earth', as the existing ground was rather too shapeless in form to be utilized. Digging in pure chalk proved to be as serious an undertaking as quarrying in stone, but the excavated material was re-used to form an embankment for a lower rose garden. As she wrote in *Gardens for Small Country Houses*, the rose garden, with rising ground on all sides but the south, appears to be sunk: it 'is a long, level green parallelogram, quiet and restful, where before [it] was only tumbled and disordered futility.' The centrepiece of the terrace is a square lily tank, and at the western end of the

terrace is a circular lily tank backed by a circular retaining wall, 6 to 7 feet high. 'The top is rather boldly planted with yuccas, the great *Euphorbia wulfenii*, cistus, tamarisk, and tree lupine,' and behind that, boxwood, broom, and red cedar.

Between the various levels, drystone walls were planted with lavender, rosemary, santolina, stonecrops, campanulas, and other sun-loving Mediterranean plants which 'rejoice in the full southern exposure and the brilliant, unveiled light of the high elevation.' From the lower terrace one could look up to the house and the long pergola flanked by garden houses, and above that, to a garden of spring flowers, such as wall-flowers, iberis, alyssum, and other plants that thrived in the lime soil. On one of the levels above the rose terrace, a long green walk offered an opportunity for colour borders with 'a massing of strong reds and yellows in the middle of the length, with the ends cooler coloured in a way that seems to make the most satisfactory colour picture,' she wrote. Another, smaller walk was dedicated to yellows and brilliant blues. 'These colour-schemes are not only highly satisfactory

Above: Drystone walls at Highmount are planted with campanula, lavender, rosemary, santolina, and other fragrant, sun-loving plants.

in themselves, but they serve to give individuality and a quality of dignity and distinction to various portions of the garden.' Each incident offered the eye one clear picture at a time and was intensified by the copious amount of low shrubs in various shades of green in between the areas.

Jekyll's approach was at odds with what she disparagingly described as the 'general muddle and want of distinct intention that is so frequent in gardens,' and which was 'so wasteful because a place may be full of fine plants, grandly grown, but if they are mixed up without a definite scheme they only produce an unsatisfactory effect, instead of composing together into a harmonious picture.' Highmount is one of Jekyll's triumphs, where she could carry out her ideas and work with an architect whose designs for steps and other structures helped harmonize the scheme. On paper, it appears to be a complex garden, but in reality it is a brilliant response to the steep topography that was so different from the more level ground for which she is better known.

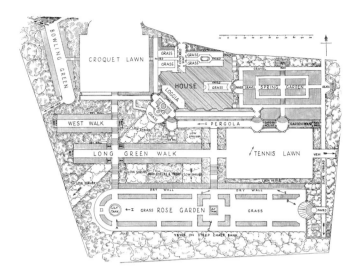

Below: *The circular lily tank at the west end of the rose garden, with steps leading up to the upper terraces on the steep site.*

Townhill Park, Hampshire

The recent rehabilitation of the formal gardens at Townhill
Park in Southampton, designed by the young architect
Leonard Rome Guthrie for Louis Samuel Montagu, 2nd Lord
Swaythling, is a wonderful addition to the roster of Jekyll
gardens that can be visited. It is another excellent expression
of the Arts and Crafts approach to design and of Jekyll's
ability to collaborate with the architect. The large formal
garden has a number of features typical of the era, such as a
pergola, a formal sunken garden, tennis lawns, and an
extensive woodland garden. Guthrie had previously enlarged
the house for Ivor Samuel Montagu, 1st Lord Swaythling,
in 1910, but after his death the following year, Guthrie
revised his plans for his son, Louis, at which point Jekyll's
assistance was sought. Guthrie, who was head draughtsman
and later partner in the office of William Flockhart, had
learned about garden design when he prepared some of the
plates for Inigo Triggs's book, *Formal Gardens in England and
Scotland* (1902). His garden designs were published in *The
Studio* and Jekyll also included Chelwood Vetchery, an earlier
project for Sir Stuart Montagu Samuel, Bt., in *Gardens for
Small Country Houses*. Guthrie's garden planning was

*Townhill Park was designed by L. Rome Guthrie in collaboration with Jekyll.
The herb garden* (top) *is on one side of the elevated pavilion and the large sunken
garden* (above), *which was once filled with masses of brightly-coloured marigolds,
is on the other side.*

Right: *A corner of the magnificent pergola which surrounds three sides of the sunken
garden is planted with wisteria, jasmine, and other climbing vines.*

strongly architectural in concept, although for Townhill Park he also laid out an informal copse and woodland walk filled with *Lilium giganteum*.

At Townhill Park, the symmetrical formal gardens on the west side of the house include terraces around the house and two tennis lawns flanked by long borders leading to a bowling green. Beyond that lay a large sunken garden surrounded on three sides by a pergola and an herb garden broken into three compartments. The planting plans that Jekyll prepared for these two areas are quite typical of her work in that they are highly detailed and somewhat illegible. Whether or not she helped plan the overall layout of the garden or offered advice on the placement of the features is unknown. The pergola that gives so much character to the garden was planted with *Wisteria sinensis*, Virginia creeper, *Clematis montana*, *Jasminum officianale*, and other climbing vines and plants that she typically used. Inside the pergola enclosure there is a cross-axial parterre garden broken into sixteen roughly triangular beds and edged with low drystone walls. Her suggestions include foxgloves, columbines, London Pride, sedum, iris, ferns, and spring-blooming plants which cascade over the walls. The colour scheme, similar to those at Millmead and Upton Grey, was one of cool colours mixed with grey foliage. For the central beds she specified masses of marigolds in bright colours, which provided a rather startling contrast. For the herb garden, which has a long walk and two compartments broken into nine beds, Jekyll specified fragrant plants, such as lavenders, rue, mint, and santolina, with pyramidal-shaped clipped yews at regular intervals. The herb garden was enclosed with low, clipped yew hedges and an old mulberry tree was in the centre. In the end Jekyll's unvarying geometric configurations were

somewhat old-fashioned, but they served her well as a foundation for her exquisite plantings.

When *Country Life* writer Randal Phillips wrote about the gardens at Townhill Park in 1923, he praised Guthrie's overall scheme, but made no mention of Jekyll's role in the sophisticated plantings which can be clearly seen in the photographs that accompany the article. After Townhill Park was sold in 1948 and the property broken up, the gardens languished for years until the site of the house and formal gardens was acquired by the Gregg and St. Winifred's Schools Trust in 1994. Three years later, a volunteer group was formed to restore the gardens, which had never been altered, although they were seriously overgrown. The sunken garden and herb gardens were refurbished and Jekyll-style herbaceous borders flanking the former tennis lawns were added. In their restoration they had to bear in mind that in Lord Swaythling's day there had been over two dozen gardeners to maintain the grounds.

After examining the original planting plans for the sunken garden, it was determined that Jekyll's scheme for brightly coloured marigolds would be far too jarring to the eye, so annuals with softer hues were substituted. The plantings in the herb garden, which were once a riot of perennials, were simplified by turning the two central beds into lawn. It was unclear whether there ever were herbaceous borders along the path, as there were neither plans nor photographs showing the area. Since Jekyll had made a name for herself with her exacting colour schemes for such borders, it was decided to plant them up. The long parallel borders were loosely modelled on those at Munstead Wood, taking into account problems with deer, weeds, and plants that have disappeared from cultivation. 'To have a good border of summer flowers, even for three months, is one of the most difficult horticultural feats,' Jekyll observed.

The borders beneath the pergola are planted with Jekyll's characteristic grey-foliage rock wall plants.

Barrington Court, Somerset

For every project that was a success, there were undoubtedly numerous ones that were a disappointment or fraught with problems. Around 1917, the architect J. Edwin Forbes, of the Forbes & Tate firm, requested Jekyll's assistance at Barrington Court in Ilminster, Somerset, where he was remodelling a house for Arthur Lyle. Colonel Lyle, who had made a fortune in the sugar refinery business (Tate & Lyle), had recently taken a 99-year lease on an old manor house dating from the 1550s and a large stable building, known as the Strode House dating from 1674. Lyle needed a home for his collection of historic wood panelling salvaged from similar manor houses, and the National Trust, which had acquired the property in 1907, was glad to offer him the opportunity to refurbish the derelict buildings for that purpose.

Forbes's master plan for the landscape was an ambitious arrangement of walled gardens, some within the original courts, while others were new, but all evoking an imaginary Elizabethan theme. Working with the architect's plan, Jekyll responded with nearly forty highly detailed drawings for a variety of themed enclosures, including a large, so-called Elizabethan garden to the east of the manor house, plus other areas dedicated to roses, peonies, and irises. She also prepared a forty-seven page proposal for thousands of plants tallying nearly £400 from her Munstead Wood nursery, which were keyed in to various compartments designated from A through R. Unfortunately, she never filled the plant order and the only areas that were implemented were those to the west of the Strode House. Colonel Lyle undoubtedly foresaw the costs in constructing and maintaining such elaborate gardens and also realized that they would have overwhelmed the architecture. Had the scheme been implemented it would have been Jekyll's largest and most important planting commission to date. Today a simplified version of her grand scheme is visible, consisting of the rose and iris garden, the lily garden, and a white garden planted in a pleasing Jekyll-esque style.

Jekyll's plans also took into consideration an old moat that partially surrounds the property. She recommended sixty-five cobnuts, as well as blackthorns, barberry, forsythia,

Above: *For the walled garden and lily pool in the old stable yard, Jekyll recommended warm-toned plants, such as dahlias and phlox.*

Left: *The former rose and peony garden at Barrington Court has been planted in a Jekyll-esque style with cream and white flowers with silver foliage.*

kerria, and large clusters of iris, monarda, forget-me-nots, and
various ferns. Many of the individual garden areas, such as
the forecourt, had elaborately clipped yew hedges, while
other areas were to be filled with her familiar, intricately
planted, colour borders. The largest and most elaborate area
was the Elizabethan Garden B, with dense flower borders
around a central grass panel consisting of heliotropes, nepeta,
asters, hollyhocks, snapdragons, clematis, and other selec-
tions, in addition to clusters of barberry, boxwood, and holly
in each of the corner angles. Sunk Garden C, which was
intended as the main garden in front of the manor house, was
an elaborate formal garden edged with double clipped yew
borders and geometric central beds flanking a central
fountain. Her planting notebook devoted seven pages to
specific plants (with prices tallied up) for this one area, such as
tree peonies, yuccas (*Yucca gloriosa* and *Y. filamentosa* in
clusters of twelve), groundcovers, clematis, lilies, and dozens
of densely planted perennials and annuals. Rose and Iris
Garden K (known as the iris garden today) was equally intensively planted, with a central sundial or vase suggested.
Walled Garden F (the lily garden today) had waterlilies in the
pool and borders overflowing with warm-toned plants, such
as fiery red and orange dahlias and phlox, and edged with
rows of *Bergenia cordifolia*. Each area was estimated to cost
anywhere from £5 to over £100.

Construction began in 1920 on a much more simplified
scheme that retained the open parkland and original orchards.
The forecourts were simplified to grass rather than being
planted up. By 1925, the lily and rose gardens were complete
based on Jekyll's plans. The rose and peony garden was the
final flower garden to be planted. When Christopher Hussey
wrote about Barrington Court in 1928, he failed to mention
the gardens. After the death of Colonel Lyle, his family
continued to work with the National Trust on developing the
gardens inspired by Jekyll's ideas, such as converting the
languishing rose and peony garden into a new garden based
on white and cream flowers with silver foliage, such as she
described in *Colour in the Flower Garden*. The family eventually bowed out in 1991 and today the property is managed
by the National Trust. Despite the disappointment of not
having the full scheme executed as she had planned, the
gardens at Barrington Court remain one of the most visible
examples of Jekyll's work in a public setting today.

*Early summer in the white garden, with wisteria trained along the enclosure walls
and borders filled with iris and other herbaceous plants favoured by Jekyll.*

Mount Stewart, Co. Down

Jekyll's name is often associated with one of the most famous gardens in the world, Mount Stewart in Newtownards, Co. Down. It is considered worthy of a horticultural pilgrimage because of its incomparable setting, enviable climate, and dazzling array of impeccably maintained gardens. The gardens covering nearly 80 acres were created by Edith, Lady Londonderry in the early 1920s. They range from woodlands and walks to themed areas, such as a Spanish garden, Italian garden, and numerous other breathtaking creations reflecting her world travels, but Jekyll played a limited role. In 1920, around the same time as she was working on Barrington Court, Jekyll prepared several plans for developing the area to the north west of the house, but the only one that Lady Londonderry adopted is a square sunken garden. Enclosed on three sides by a hedge of *Cupressus*

macrocarpa and a stone pergola covered in soft yellow *Lonicera etrusca* and *Rosa gigantea*, the garden is best viewed from the west front of the elegant Georgian house. It was planted in hot tones, with yellows on one side and reds on the other, somewhat similar to the lily garden at Barrington Court. Luxuriant waves of warm-toned flowers punctuated with deep blue are set off by a rich green lawn which provides the perfect foil for the grey stone terrace and the cool, grey climate of Northern Ireland. Some of the plants include vivid orange Ghent azaleas (*Azalea* 'Coccinea Speciosa'), yellow tree lupins and roses, blue clematis, anchusa, ceanothus, and *Lithospermum*, and purple violas.

Above: *The sunken garden at Mount Stewart is enclosed by a cypress hedge and stone pergola.*

Photographs published by *Country Life* in 1928 show densely planted borders along the stone retaining wall for the pergola, and borders flanking the green lawn below that. There are four curved-edged borders on the lawn (now reconfigured) and at each of the four corners a stone surround with a Norway maple (now the copper-leaved *Acer platanoides* 'Crimson King'). Around 1970, the National Trust's gardens advisor, Graham Stuart Thomas, helped restore the garden to its former magnificence after the death of Lady Londonderry; in more recent years it has been looked after by Nigel Marshall. Lady Londonderry's original colour scheme for blue, yellow, and orange in the sunken garden has been augmented with many new herbaceous perennials as substitutes for the earlier labour-intensive annuals. Mount Stewart's sunken garden remains an excellent example of Jekyll's timeless ideas about colour in the garden.

Above: *The west front of the Georgian house overlooks the sunken garden, the only area where Jekyll's suggestions were implemented.*

Below: *A corner of the sunken garden, with a stone pergola covered in roses and* Lonicera etrusca, *and borders filled with warm-toned flowers and deep blue.*

Durford Edge, Hampshire

Jekyll was never busier than in the mid-1920s when she was in her late seventies. Not only was she writing dozens of articles, but she was also advising on eight to ten new gardens a year in addition to her long-term involvement with Lutyens's Gledstone Hall. By 1929, this pace had tapered off, but in 1932, the year she died, she was engaged on at least one garden. One typical example from this period is Durford Edge in Petersfield, Hampshire. John Percy Gabbatt, a professor of mathematics, asked Jekyll to design a garden for a house that had been built in 1911 by Unsworth and Triggs. Inigo Triggs ranked high in Jekyll's estimation, namely for his books as well as his gardens at Little Boarhunt, which she featured in *Gardens for Small Country Houses*. When she received the garden commission from Dr Gabbatt in 1923, however, Triggs was no longer with the firm and died in April that year.

As was typical of her working methods, the architects supplied several plans of proposed garden layouts, as well as thirty-one photographs showing various aspects of the house and sloping terrain. Jekyll responded with her suggestions, beginning in March 1923 and worked on and off on the designs until September 1926. The proposed gardens looped along the front and side in one long, curved terrace with low drystone walls. Several different configurations were suggested, but what was eventually built included a circular pool garden with a central elevated statue on a post (similar to the design at Little Boarhunt), and a rill connecting the garden to the steps leading up to the house. A companion rill, with semicircular tanklets, similar to those at Hestercombe, came off another axis. A sketch was sent for a round rose garden to include *Rosa* 'Mrs Ed Powell', 'La Tosca', 'Lady Hillingdon', 'Richmond', 'Mme Abel Chatenay', and others. Jekyll's plans included ideas for an azalea garden, an orchard, a large formal garden with flowering shrub borders, and numerous wall plantings. She drew up extensive plant lists in her job notebook and enquired with Godalming Nurseries if they could supply some of the plants as well. In all it was an ideal small country house garden and the owner was quite pleased with the result. 'With thanks again for all you have done for us,' Dr. Gabbatt wrote in 1926.

Above: *The terrace gardens at Durford Edge followed the line of the house, with a circular pool and a rill.*

Right: *The statue on a post in the pool was similar to the one at Little Boarhunt for Inigo Triggs.*

Woodhouse Copse, Surrey

With the young architect Oliver Hill, Jekyll enjoyed both a devoted friendship and an ideal working partnership. By the early 1920s, Hill had made a name for himself as a young architect of promise and like his mentor, Edwin Lutyens, his work was regularly featured in *Country Life*, in a new series called 'Lesser Country Houses of To-Day' under the authorship of Randal Phillips. Like Lutyens, he had a natural talent for designing gardens that perfectly complemented his houses, beginning at Moor Close in 1910 with a new water garden adorned with a handsome pergola and pavilion.

Hill, whose mother collected Jekyll's books, first met her at one of her sister-in-law Lady Agnes Jekyll's weekend parties at Munstead House, and from that moment on, Hill wrote, he sat at her feet for the rest of her life. 'Although I held her in the utmost respect, I suffered acute fear of boring her, but she was kindness itself.' They went on to collaborate on no fewer than five gardens, including one for his weekend cottage at Valewood Farm. As a young man, Hill had fallen under the influence of *Country Life* magazine and through Lawrence Weaver he was introduced to Lutyens and soon made expeditions to Munstead Wood, Deanery Garden, Lindisfarne, and Marsh Court, as well as several of Harold Peto's commissions.

In 1924, Amy Barnes-Brand, an actress (under the name Miss Amy Brandon-Thomas), engaged Hill to remodel a modest cottage in Holmbury St. Mary, Surrey, called Woodhouse Copse, and two years later Jekyll was invited to assist with the gardens. The original thatched cottage, which harked back to an earlier era in English domestic architecture, was built of timber, brick, and stone. Hill incorporated a massive post from an old windmill in the centre of a new spiral staircase. Jekyll's first collaboration with Hill had been

a town garden at Wilbraham House in London in 1922, followed a year later by a garden at Fox Steep in Wargrave-on-Thames, where Hill had remodelled the house. The commission at Woodhouse Copse is unusual for the amount of surviving correspondence, and like Hill, Amy Barnes-Brand was familiar with Jekyll's books. The basic layout for the garden was provided by Hill when he fashioned the eclectic house. Like Munstead Wood, the main living room overlooked the garden and the woodlands beyond. A pergola extended from the house to a gazebo on one side, with a curious pool lined with blue mosaic. A series of semicircular intersecting steps, similar to those at Hestercombe and Deanery Garden, links the terraces near the house with the lower grass terraces.

Jekyll's charge was to design flower borders, an activity at which she excelled in the 1920s when she was rarely laying out whole gardens herself. The main borders were set between yew hedges on falling ground leading to a stream and a small woodland garden. She felt that the double borders at Woodhouse Copse, which were 63 feet in length, were 'rather too short to give a really good effect.' In her letter that accompanied her plans, she gave detailed instructions for maintaining the borders and using *Clematis flammula* to cover delphiniums when out of flower. She wisely rejected her client's ideas for including spring bulbs in the borders, having learned from her own experience in her first border at Munstead House in the 1880s that their dying foliage is unsightly. As was the case for many of her commissions, the recommended plants were dispatched from her nursery at Munstead Wood. Her planting plans, drawn up between October 1926 and September 1928, covered plantings for the drystone walls, a water garden, peony and iris borders, and a rose garden, as well as fruit trees and roses for the orchard. In all it was a splendid garden that did justice to Hill's whimsical house.

Above: *The quaint thatched cottage at Woodhouse Copse provided a backdrop for flower borders. A series of semicircular steps links the house to the grass terraces below.*

Right: *Jekyll's first collaboration with Oliver Hill was a town garden at Wilbraham House, London, in 1922.*

Valewood Farm, Surrey

Valewood Farm, Oliver Hill's romantic weekend retreat near Haslemere in Surrey, had the most enchanting of his gardens, of which nothing remains today. The quaintness and remoteness of the picturesque old yeoman's house was captured in the early 1900s in several paintings by Helen Allingham long before Hill acquired the derelict property in the 1920s. Randal Phillips, writing in 1928, pointed out that Hill's renovation of the cottage, its furnishing, and the layout of the garden 'clearly proclaim the hand of an architect who is also an artist.' One can only imagine Jekyll's delight in assisting the architect with his own garden. 'It was she who schemed the planting plan, and gave many plants from her own garden,' he wrote. In a feature for *Country Life* in 1935, Christopher Hussey also acknowledged Jekyll's role at Valewood Farm, noting that 'The garden is a small but notable example of the "impressionistic" style associated with Miss Jekyll, who, indeed supplied the original planting plan for the main beds.' It is unfortunate that those plans have gone missing, but the wealth of period photographs clearly show the impact of her ideas and the fruits of her collaborative effort with the architect in bringing about a most unusual garden. 'The whole was

a little work of art,' wrote Hussey, 'part garden and part sheer fairy-story.'

The fairy story is evident in some of Hill's touches throughout the garden, in particular the menagerie of resident peacocks, doves, parrots, geese, and budgerigars. The principal garden was laid out in a swampy old farmyard between the house and an old barn. A clipped beech hedge separates the forecourt of the house from the barn garden. The centrepiece of the barn garden is an oval bathing pool filled with blue water (created by adding handfuls of copper sulphate crystals to discourage vegetation), overlooked by a pair of life-size verdigris green Pompeiian fawns. Opposite the pool is a covered loggia and changing alcove on one side and across the lawn another vine-covered loggia, all serving to enclose the garden space.

Hussey commended the garden for the pictorial use made of ordinary plants and common materials, such as the low walls

Above: *Oliver Hill's weekend retreat, Valewood Farm, had picturesque, cottage-style gardens.*

Right: *Jekyll's impressionistic planting style suited the yeoman's cottage.*

surrounding the house planted with rosemary and the towering junipers flanking the doorway. The cool silver-grey colour of the stone on the lower part of the house and the warm russet of the weather-tiled walls and the roof are echoed throughout the garden. The herbaceous borders at the foot of the stone walls have been designed with a predominantly blue colour scheme, 'with masses of delphiniums, anchusas and *Salvia virgata*, relieved by pink sidalcea and grey foliage-plants,' all of which harmonized with the blue of the bathing pool, to quote Hussey. Beside the pool Hill placed a large green-glazed oil jar and white tubs filled with blue agapanthus. Beyond the barn, a walkway leads through plantings that were predominantly evergreens interspersed with masses of lupins, gorse, broom, lilacs, and beech, and a couple of ornamental cow parsleys ('a noxious but handsome weed that has to be keep under careful control,' observed Hussey).

For a weekend garden, Valewood required constant maintenance and over the years, prior to Hill's departure to Daneway House in Gloucestershire, the general nature of it changed, but still retained the delicate balance of formality and informality which was one of the hallmarks of Jekyll's teachings. Jekyll worked on one more project for Hill late in 1929, a new sandstone house in Hurtwood, Surrey, named Marylands, a Mediterranean-inspired villa which also took its cue from Lutyens's work at Lindisfarne. By this time Hill was closing the chapter on his Arts and Crafts-vernacular style and moving toward Modernism, which earned him the apt soubriquet 'Chameleon' by Alan Powers.

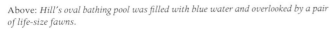

Above: *Hill's oval bathing pool was filled with blue water and overlooked by a pair of life-size fawns.*
Right: *Peacocks on the roof of the open dining loggia were part of Hill's menagerie.*

Garden Ornament

· · · · · · · · · · · ·

"Many a garden of formal design is spoilt by a multiplicity and variety of ornament."

· · · · · · · · · · · ·

An antique wellhead and column in front of the pavilion at Iford Manor, Harold Peto's home in Wiltshire.

The subject of garden ornament never failed to elicit Jekyll's most critical comments, whether a garden bench painted the wrong colour, gate piers choked with ivy, or a sundial misplaced on a terrace. Her ideas on the subject ran through several of her books, but in 1918 Country Life published *Garden Ornament*, an oversize folio filled with full-plate illustrations, in the hope that it would 'quicken the interest in beautiful gardening [and] show how ornament may best be applied, according to the quality or caliber of any place.' Brief descriptions and critical remarks about both good and bad examples of ornament were offered in the hope of assisting in 'the preservation of harmony and avoidance of incongruity.'

In 1927, Jekyll collaborated with Christopher Hussey on a second edition filled with fresh pictures and comments, some of which contradicted those of the earlier one.

Jekyll began writing about garden ornament as early as 1911, when she published two articles in *Country Life* about its historical relevance. In a nod to her deep knowledge of the history of the subject, she wryly observed that few features of consequence emerged during the Tudor era, with the exception of ornamental parterres and knot gardens, both of which lent an unsatisfactory sense of cramped space, rather than freedom. It wasn't until the classically-inspired ideals of the Italian Renaissance spread to England in the early sixteenth century that garden design began to have an intellectual model. In keeping with the precepts of the ancient world, the garden was considered as an extension of the house, rather than as a separate entity. From the sixteenth century onwards gardens were largely designed by architects and so began to be lavishly embellished with architectural ornament.

English architects who embraced these ideals created some of the great houses of the English Renaissance, such as Hardwick Hall, Wollaton, and Longleat and with them adaptations of the gardens of the Italian Renaissance, which left its

At Folly Farm, Berkshire, Edwin Lutyens's circular steps provide a playful contrast with the herringbone-brick terrace. One of his signature benches is tucked into the hedged alcove overlooking the rose garden.

legacy in a reverence for water and its fountains, cisterns, and pools. But translation to Britain was fraught with problems. 'Nothing is more frequent than to see some garden pool or fountain basin with a little water in the bottom only,' Jekyll wrote, 'and nothing looks worse or more neglectful.' She was ever-vigilant about misuse of features and bad scale in gardens. 'The Italian garden designers of the fifteenth century … showed an astonishing boldness of conception and fertility of invention. The whole thing was done with a kind of passion [that] came straight out of the artist's mind.' On the other hand, the English will 'import a Venetian *pozzo* and put it as a centre ornament *on gravel* in the middle of a hybrid parterre in an open garden, where the poor exile cries aloud for its old environment of wall-encompassed courtyard and flagged pavement; or, if we are more ambitious, we bring over a pair of highly-decorated marble vases and erect them on plain plinths with a very slight and thin moulding at the base, as an ornament to the top of a short flight of unmoulded garden steps!'

Jekyll's stinging comments about the misuse of ornament were often balanced with praise for simple things well done, such as the wooden gate 'of excellent design' at Cleeve Prior Manor. 'Painted white, it shows up well against the background of yews.' But her highest praise was always reserved for Lutyens, whose steps at Hestercombe she singled out for their 'brilliant effect of light and shade.'

Garden Houses

Small garden structures, which had traditionally offered shelter from the weather or provided a comfortable space for afternoon tea and other leisure activities, were a popular ornamental component in country house gardens. 'The success of summer-houses and pavilions, considered as elements of garden design, depends as much upon their skilful placing as upon their form and materials,' Jekyll and Weaver stated in *Gardens for Small Country Houses*. Whatever their style, location, or materials, it was essential that pavilions and other built elements should be harmonious with the overall architecture, yet not dominate it. Sometimes these pavilions were connected to a pergola, in which case the architectural treatment needed to be compatible. For example, L. Rome Guthrie's porticoed loggia at Townhill Park is smothered in the same vines as the connecting pergola. Sometimes a simple gazebo at the corner of a terrace provided

architectural interest as well as a resting place from the sun. Inigo Triggs's modest garden at Little Boarhunt included a charming garden house perched in one corner of the walled enclosure. It was not only an attractive focal point for the garden, but also a design opportunity to reinforce the architectural style of the house. Lutyens often provided garden houses and gazebos to emphasize the geometry of his early houses and gardens, but the true master of pavilion design was Harold Peto, whose elegant buildings served as a focal point for his magnificent water gardens. Rustic shelters, made from logs and with thatched roofs, were perfect for children's gardens.

Above: *L. Rome Guthrie's elegant loggia at Townhill Park, Hampshire, provides a fine focal point for the formal gardens.*

Right: *A perfectly scaled garden house in the corner of Inigo Triggs's small garden at Little Boarhunt, Hampshire.*

Pergolas

Pergolas were one of the most prevalent features in the country house garden, but as an import from Italy they did not make a significant impact on English gardens until architects picked up the idea in the late nineteenth century. As a design feature, pergolas offered an attractive method of enclosing the garden, providing shade, or linking areas or other features, such as garden pavilions. They also provided a framework for growing all sorts of climbing vines. In Jekyll's time, there was scarcely a modern garden without a pergola, but most in her opinion were 'injudiciously placed'. In those gardens which 'have not had the benefit of experienced advice,' she wrote, the 'poorly constructed pergola stands in some open place where it has no obvious beginning or end;

whereas it should always lead from one definite point to another.' Pergolas could be a mere framework of poles (which needed to be replaced on a regular basis) or more solidly built of masonry. In British gardens, Jekyll argued, the posts are best made of oak trunks with the bark stripped off and coated with tar. After setting up the posts, slighter logs are spiked to each pair of posts across the path, taking care with any slight curvatures of the log. 'Nothing looks weaker or less satisfactory than a cross-beam that swags downwards.'

The best pergolas, in Jekyll's opinion, were those designed by architects and garden designers who understood both design and horticulture. Depending on the architectural style, they could be constructed of ordinary brick with mortar joints, or in the case of Lutyens, alternating round and square

Left: *Peto's magnificent pergola at Easton Lodge, Essex, is enhanced with delicate* treillage *and lush plantings; in contrast, the rustic pergola and walkway (above) at Great Tangley Manor, Surrey, is constructed of rough poles.*

piers built of tiles with wide joints, such as those at Deanery Garden, Hestercombe, Little Thakeham, and Tigbourne Court. Equally attractive was Avray Tipping's simple stone pergola adjacent to a pool at Mounton House, which depended for its effect on luxuriant overgrowth. Jekyll reserved her highest praise for Peto's pergolas in England and the South of France, such as the magnificent examples at the Countess of Warwick's Easton Lodge in Essex, and at Villa Rosemary, Saint-Jean-Cap-Ferrat, as showing the 'highest expression of architectural refinement.' She felt Peto fully understood the principles of good design and placement, and besides was an excellent horticulturist who knew the effects that could be achieved with a careful selection of plants.

The most successful pergolas, according to Jekyll, are those built on level ground and straight from end to end, but sometimes they can follow flights of steps and landings. In any case, the path beneath should always be paved in order to avoid a muddy track. Pergolas, of course, offer endless horticultural opportunities for growing all sorts of vines, such as

grapevines, Virginia creeper, wisteria, clematis, jasmine, honeysuckle, and roses, the latter requiring great care in pruning and training. For roses it is preferable to have a succession of piers and beams only so that they can have the benefit of light and air all round. The addition of chains hanging from post to post could be used to form garlands, but 'all gardeners who have had to do with rose garlands know the trouble of the whole thing swinging round to the under side, like a saddle turning on a horse.' Great care should be taken in selecting plantings for beneath the pergola because of the shady situation and nothing is more striking than lines of white lilies.

Above: Lutyens's pergola at Hestercombe, Somerset, consists of alternating round and square piers built of local shale.

Right: The waterlily pool at Avray Tipping's Mounton House, Monmouthshire, is offset with a simple pergola profusely covered with rambler roses.

Paving, walls, and steps

Paved courtyards and terraces, which lent definition to separate areas within the garden, were one of the hallmarks of formal country gardens. Avray Tipping found paved courtyards essential for offering shelter in his exposed Monmouthshire gardens, such as the one at Mounton House. But from Jekyll's viewpoint paved courtyards and terraces raised the question of the proper ratio of plants to an architectural framework, and with entrance courts in particular she felt that the plantings should not be overdone. For the architect, these spaces offered endless opportunities for variations in paving patterns and materials, ranging from rustic brick and cobblestones to smooth York pavers. Lutyens's penchant for geometry often took on a life of its own when applied to paving details. He combined brick laid in a herringbone pattern and York pavers for decorative interest, as well as a unifying feature throughout the garden. At Hestercombe, Jekyll commended his use of paving along the edges of grass walks because they not only provided a dry footway but also prevented the lawn mower from damaging plants.

Most gardens of the era were at least partially enclosed by high walls as well as low drystone ones to accommodate any slope of the ground. Ideally they should be built of local materials similar to those used for the house. In the Cotswolds, for example, walls were roughly constructed of local honey-coloured limestone, whereas in Surrey Bargate stone lent a slightly more formal effect. As she wrote in *Wall and Water Gardens*, drywalls, such as those at Millmead and The Manor House at Upton Grey, provided endless planting opportunities for rock plants. Informal groups of silvery saxifrages, santolinas, and cerastium could be mixed with more showy flowers and even small shrubs. Drywalls, of course, needed to be constructed properly so that proper drainage was ensured: 'In making the dry-walling the stones should all tip a little downwards at the back and the whole face of the wall should incline slightly backward, so that no drop of rain is lost, but all runs into the joints.'

High enclosure walls lent a distinct architectural note, especially if they served to connect the house with the gardens. Most of Lutyens's gardens were enclosed with walls that echoed the architectural style of the house and ancillary buildings, such as garden shelters and gate houses. Typically there were arched openings connecting one area to another. Lutyens's majestic archways ornamented with sunbursts made with tiles laid on end were one of his signatures, such as the handsome arch in the kitchen gardens at Orchards. For a more informal appearance, walls could be covered in vines or espaliered fruit trees, as Jekyll did at Munstead Wood.

Top: *Steep steps in a hillside garden at Hurtwood, Surrey, are flanked by dramatic planters at each landing.*

Above: *Lutyens's semicircular steps in each of the four corners of the great plat at Hestercombe, Somerset.*

Opposite (above): *The grass walkways at Hestercombe are paved along the edges to protect the plants.*
(below): *Lutyens used slate-on-edge paving under the pavilions at Gledstone Hall, Yorkshire.*

Another feature beloved by architects of the period were steps, whether an uninterrupted long flight from one level to the next, or semicircular steps at the corners of flat parterres. Sometimes Lutyens overdid the interplay of circular and square steps, but they added immensely to the character of his gardens. Other architects picked up on the ornamental value of steps, imitating to a certain extent what Lutyens had done so well. Jekyll, of course, was concerned about the correct height of the steps and also the play of light and dark between the treads and risers. 'The decorative value of steps consists primarily in the alternation of horizontal bands of light and shade – shining treads and dark risers [and] if this is borne in mind, the right proportion of rise to tread will follow naturally,' she wrote in *Garden Ornament*. One should also keep in mind that there is a point where the spectator tends to halt and survey the view. 'Excessive perfection of work-manship produces a hard appearance,' she noted. 'Perfect examples of rough stepping made with great slabs of stone are seen at Hestercombe.'

Above: *The enclosed terrace and archway in the wall at Tipping's Mounton House, Monmouthshire.*

Opposite: *Ernest Gimson's whimsical dovecote in the stone wall at his house in Sapperton, Gloucestershire.*

Below (left): *Lutyens's rusticated gateway into the 'Dutch' garden at Hestercombe, Somerset.*
(right): *A glimpse into the kitchen garden through the archway at Orchards, Surrey.*

Water features

Ranging from naturalistic stream gardens to paved terraces with tanks, water features provided endless opportunities for horticultural embellishment. One of the most prevalent forms was the lily pool filled with many new varieties of waterlilies that were just becoming available in Britain. 'These grand plants enable us to compose a whole series of new pictures of plant beauty of the highest order,' Jekyll wrote in *Wall and Water Gardens*. William Robinson, for example, had a small tank in his paved garden at Gravetye dedicated to new French introductions by M. Latour Marliac, such as *Nymphaea marliacea albida* (white) and *N. m. Chromatella* (pale yellow). In addition, tanks might be planted with a whole range of other water-loving plants, such as arums, water forget-me-nots, and water plantains, but care needed to be taken that they were planted correctly, did not become too overwhelming, and were kept away from the edges of the tanks. Peto, who was the era's consummate architect-plantsman, had special ways of combining various water-

loving plants in pools with groupings of ornamental shrubs and vines along the paved terraces.

Formal water gardens lent themselves to a variety of shapes and configurations, from circular, fan-shaped, or rectangular tanks to that 'capital invention', the paved rill, which was used so successfully by Lutyens at Hestercombe. 'Pools and rills, when in close connection with house or terrace wall, give the architect an opportunity of carrying out [an] orna-mental design [such as] a tank, circular in plan and a half circle in elevation notched in under the building.' Pools and tanks might form part of a more elaborate water system, whereby the water trickled from a spouting masque into a pool, then ran along a rill to a collecting tank. Fountain masques and ornamental sculptural figures further enriched

Above: *Harold Peto was a consummate planting artist. In the canal garden at Bridge House, Surrey, the delicate waterlilies contrast with the drooping hydrangea and the lushly festooned pergola.*

the water garden. Jekyll exhorted that care needed to be taken about the 'proper relation of the water-level to the edge of the tank, [a] matter that is often overlooked.' Not only was too little water unsightly, but most tanks were needlessly deep – they needn't be more than 2 feet deep. 'If a basin of water forms a definite part of a garden scheme the line of the water at the right height is as important as any other line in the design.'

Above right: *At Hestercombe, water from the spouting masque under the terrace drips into a circular pool, then runs along a channel to collect in a square holding tank* (below) *near the pergola.*

Sculptural ornament

Decorative features, such as urns and cast figures, found a prominent place in country house gardens, but they needed to be used sparingly in small gardens, Jekyll cautioned, so as to not overwhelm the design. If well placed, however, they added immeasurably to the scheme. Traditional cherubs and the like were quite acceptable, but more favoured in Jekyll gardens were ornamental figures designed by contemporary sculptors, such as Lady Chance. Not only did she design the lion's head masque in her fountain at Orchards, but also the imaginative spouting lead *hippocampi* ('a delightful beast, spouting from his muzzle') surrounding the tank at Marsh Court, as well as a line of lead tortoises that literally dance about the pool at Heywood House in Co. Laois, Ireland.

Antique cisterns, bird baths, pumps, and well-heads were popular as well, but sundials were one of the most prevalent ornamental features of the day. 'Care should be taken about the proper placing of a sundial,' whether as a central object in a parterre or in the middle of a grass plat or at the end of a path, Jekyll advised. Sundials depend more for their decorative success on 'their right placing than on their intrinsic merit as garden sculpture.' She wryly commented, 'it is not unusual to see an old shaft and dial, that no doubt had been formerly well placed, put out on a lawn in haphazard way, looking forlorn and as if it had lost its way.' Wherever it is placed, however, it requires at least one stone step, and two steps would be better; it should also have some kind of base that 'will give it due emphasis and importance.' One such example is the sundial at Gravetye Manor designed in a twisted baluster pattern by Sir Ernest George, which Jekyll described as follows: 'It is set on a moulded square base, which rises from an octagonal platform. Simple and slender as it is, it has an air of dignity by reason of being properly set.'

Right: *Julia Chance's lion's head masque in the tile-built fountain at Orchards, Surrey.*

Below (left): *Ernest George's sundial on the terrace at Gravetye Manor, Sussex, is traditional in form and placement.*
(right): *Lutyens copied the detailing of the chalk and flint house at Marsh Court, Hampshire, in the sundial in the courtyard.*

Above: *Rising from the boxwood cubes, individual lead fountains in the shape of* hippocampi *spout water from their muzzles in the sunken terrace of Marsh Court, Hampshire.*

Left: *Lead garden ornaments (tortoise, toad,* hippocampus, *and dolphin) designed by Julia Chance.*

Right: *Tortoises designed by Julia Chance dance around the circular pool at Heywood, Abbeyleix.*

Hedges and topiary

Architectural interest in the garden could also be created with living walls of hedges, whether planted in straight lines or clipped in fanciful shapes. Majestic yews that give so much character to old places, such as Owlpen Manor and Cleeve Prior, require caution in a small, modern garden. Traditional long, clipped hedges also form a framework for the flower borders at their feet and architects, of course, loved the idea of using yews to add drama to their garden schemes. Ilex, beech, and hornbeam serve equally well, but whatever the plant, the clipping must be done by hand and not with shears. Fine effects can also be had with upright trees linked together, such as Lombardy poplars. 'As in the case of other toy-like tricks in gardening, it may in some cases be satisfactorily employed, but if followed merely as a fashion, and not because the design of the garden would be bettered by a certain form, it may easily give an impression of silliness or wanton frivolity.'

Jekyll was cautious in her use of topiary, considering it somewhat of a holdover from an earlier era, although she did

Top: *A pair of whimsical topiaries on the terrace at Tigbourne Court, Surrey.*

Above: *A fanciful garden shelter at Tipping's Mathern Palace, Monmouthshire, formed with clipped yews and replete with arches and window openings.*

Right: *The grass allée at Mathern Palace is lined with a double row of yews clipped into bird forms.*

have a topiary cat on the lawn at Munstead Wood made by clipping a single yew which suggested a feline shape. William Robinson, of course, had no patience with the practice of clipping trees into unnatural forms. Jekyll cited the amusing example of a hypothetical man who is not much of a gardener, but fancies himself an architect and decides to fill up an empty yard with clipped yews, which can be planted easily and come in all forms from cones to peacocks. 'They suddenly give an air of completion to his garden – a few days' hard work can turn the muddy levels into something quite like a garden.' A regiment of clipped yews dotted over the garden produce a spotty effect, as in endless examples of large Victorian estates.

On the other side of the coin, 'given judicious use, nothing forms a better frame for a house and garden than topiary.' A good example is the treatment of the long yew hedges at Tipping's early garden at Mathern Palace. The yews are trained up in the form of swollen cones surmounted by bird forms. 'In unpractised hands such treatment might be dangerous, but in that of Mathern's owner we know that his skill and fine taste will bring them into right and fitting garden ornaments.'

Flower borders

The icing on the cake for many country house gardens was Jekyll's signature flower borders and those designed by her followers. As she demonstrated so well at Munstead Wood, one should not attempt too much or use too many different plants in a border. Borders also need lead plants with a supporting chorus to reinforce the intended look. Flower borders ranged from the billowing informality that was so suited to Oliver Hill's cottage garden at Valewood to the high-maintenance exhibition borders at Folly Farm. Jekyll's finely-tuned sense of colour and texture was hard to replicate, but her serious followers used her principles as a starting point for their own personal planting style, as Avray Tipping demonstrates in his walled garden at Mounton House.

Jekyll showed the way for the ornamental value of well-planted borders to complement water features, or emphasize the rustication of drystone walls, or take one's breath away in dazzling patterns in parterres. It had taken years to formulate her theories and she acknowledged that there had been many failures in the process. As she wrote in *Colour in the Flower*

Above: *Jekyll's glorious main flower border at Munstead Wood was a symphony of textural contrasts and a precise arrangement of colours.*

Left: *Oliver Hill's cottage-style borders and rustic pergola at Valewood Farm, Surrey.*

Garden, 'nothing seems to me more unsatisfactory than the border that in spring shows a few patches of flowering bulbs in ground otherwise looking empty, or with tufts of herbaceous plants just coming through. Then the bulbs die down, and their place is wanted for something that comes later. Either the ground will then show bare patches, or the place of the bulbs will be forgotten and they will be cruelly stabbed by fork or trowel when it is wished to put something in the apparently dead space.' She acknowledged that she had given a great deal of thought to methods of arranging flowers, 'especially in ways of colour-combinations.' At Munstead Wood and in all her garden commissions, she used plants to 'form beautiful pictures'. Every plant or group of plants needs to be placed with thoughtful care and definite intention so that they shall form a part of a 'harmonious whole' and 'show a series of pictures'.

Jekyll also set the record straight on the difference between commonplace gardening and that which could be ranked as a fine art. 'Given the same space of ground and the same material [plants] may either be fashioned into a dream of beauty, a place of perfect rest and refreshment of mind and body – a series of soul-satisfying pictures – a treasure of well-set jewels; or they may be so misused that everything is jarring and displeasing. To learn how to perceive the difference and how to do right is to apprehend gardening as a fine art.'

Above: *Tipping's paved garden at Mounton House, Monmouthshire, has dense borders and a wall necessary for shelter from the prevailing winds.*

Right: *The grand flower parterre at Folly Farm, Berkshire, which was later simplified by Lanning Roper. The network of beds is offset with Lutyens's rustic herringbone-brick paths.*

Bibliography

BOOKS

Amery, Colin, et al., *Lutyens: The Work of the English Architect Sir Edwin Lutyens (1869-1944)*, Arts Council of Great Britain, London, 1981.

Aslet, Clive, *The Last Country Houses*, Yale University Press, London and New York, 1982.

Beetles, Chris, *Art and Sunshine: The Work of Hercules Brabazon Brabazon, 1821–1906*, Chris Beetles Ltd., London, 1997.

Benson, A. C., and Weaver, Lawrence, eds., *The Book of the Queen's Dolls' House*, 2 vols., Methuen, London, 1924.

Bisgrove, Richard, *The Gardens of Gertrude Jekyll*, Frances Lincoln, London, 1992.

—, *William Robinson: The Wild Gardener*, Frances Lincoln, London, 2008.

Blomfield, Reginald, *The Formal Garden in England*, Macmillan, London, 1892.

Brown, Jane, *The Art and Architecture of English Gardens*, Rizzoli, New York, 1989.

—, *Gardens of a Golden Afternoon, The Story of a Partnership: Edwin Lutyens and Gertrude Jekyll*, Penguin, London, 1982 .

—, *The English Garden through the 20th Century*, Garden Art Press, Woodbridge, 1999.

—, *Lutyens and the Edwardians: An English Architect and His Clients*, Viking, London, 1950.

Budgen, Christopher, *West Surrey Architecture: 1840–2000*, Heritage of Waverley, Woking, 2002.

Butler, A. S. G., *The Architecture of Sir Edwin Lutyens (The Lutyens Memorial)*, Country Life, London, 1950.

Cook, E. T., ed., *The Century Book of Gardening*, Country Life, London, 1900.

Cornforth, John, *The Inspiration of the Past: Country House Taste in the Twentieth Century*, Viking, London, 1985.

—, *The Search for a Style: Country Life and Architecture, 1897–1935*, André Deutsch, London, 1988.

Crossly, Alan; Hassall, Tom; and Salway, Peter, eds., *William Morris's Kelmscott: Landscape and History*, Windgather Press, Macclesfield, 2007.

Darwin, Bernard, *Fifty Years of 'Country Life'*, Country Life, London, 1947.

Davey, John, ed. *Nature and Tradition: Arts and Crafts Architecture and Gardens In and Around Guildford*, Surrey Gardens Trust, Guildford, 1993.

Elgood, George S., and Jekyll, Gertrude, *Some English Gardens*, Longmans, London, 1904.

Elliott, Brent, *The Country House Garden: From the Archives of Country Life, 1897–1939*, Mitchell Beazley, London, 1995.

Gow, Ian, *Scottish Houses and Gardens: From the Archives of Country Life*, Aurum Press, London, 1997.

Gradidge, Roderick, *Dream Houses: The Edwardian Ideal*, Constable, London, 1980.

—, *Edwin Lutyens: Architect Laureate*, George Allen & Unwin, London, 1981.

—, *The Surrey Style*, Surrey Historic Buildings Trust, Godalming, 1991.

Greensted, Mary, *The Arts and Crafts Movement in the Cotswolds*, Sutton, Stroud, 1993.

Gunn, Fenja, *Lost Gardens of Gertrude Jekyll*, Letts, London, 1991.

Hall, Michael, *The English Country House: From the Archives of Country Life, 1897–1939*, Aurum Press, London, 2001.

Hamilton, Jill; Hart, Penny; and Simmons, John, *The Gardens of William Morris*, Frances Lincoln, London, 1998.

Hayward, Allyson, *Norah Lindsay: The Life and Art of a Garden Designer*, Frances Lincoln, London, 2007.

Hobhouse, Penelope, and Wood, Christopher, *Painted Gardens: English Watercolours, 1850–1914*, Pavilion Books, London, 1988.

Holme, Charles, ed., *The Gardens of England in the Midland and Eastern Counties, The Gardens of England in the Northern Counties, The Gardens of England in the Southern and Western Counties*, The Studio, London, 1907–11.

Hussey, Christopher, *The Life of Sir Edwin Lutyens*, Country Life, London, 1950 .

—, *The Work of Sir Robert Lorimer*, Country Life, London, 1931.

Jekyll, Francis, *Gertrude Jekyll: A Memoir*, Jonathan Cape, London, 1934.

Jekyll, Gertrude, *Annuals and Biennials*, Country Life, London, 1916.

—, *Children and Gardens*, Country Life, London, 1908.

—, *Colour in the Flower Garden*, Country Life, London, 1908.

—, *Flower Decoration in the House*, Country Life, London, 1907.

—, *Home and Garden*, Longmans, London, 1900.

—, *Lilies for English Gardens*, Country Life, London, 1901.

—, *Old West Surrey*, Longmans, London, 1904.

—, *Roses for English Gardens*, Country Life, London, 1902.

—, *Wall and Water Gardens*, Country Life, London, 1901.

—, *Wood and Garden*, Longmans, London, 1899.

—, and Hussey, Christopher, *Garden Ornament*, Country Life, London, 1927.

—, and Weaver, Lawrence, *Gardens for Small Country Houses*, Country Life, London, 1912.

Le Lièvre, Audrey, *Miss Willmott of Warley Place: Her Life and Her Gardens*, Faber & Faber, London, 1980.

Leland, John, and Tipping, H. Avray, eds., *Gardens Old and New: The Country House and Its Garden Environment*, 3 vols. Country Life, London, 1901–08.

Mako, Marion, *Painting in Three Dimensions: Alfred Parsons in Broadway* (MA diss.), University of Bristol, 2004.

Mander, Nicholas, *Country Houses of the Cotswolds: From the Archives of Country Life*, Aurum Press, London, 2008.

Marsh, Jan, *William Morris and Red House*, National Trust Books, London, 2005.

Mawson, Thomas, *The Art and Craft of Garden Making*, Batsford, London, 1900.

O'Reilly, Seán, *Irish Houses and Gardens: From the Archives of Country Life*, Aurum Press, London, 1998.

Ottewill, David, *The Edwardian Garden*, Yale University Press, London, 1989.

Powers, Alan, *Oliver Hill: Architect and Lover of Life, 1887–1968*, Mouton Publications, London, 1989 .

Richardson, Margaret, *Architects of the Arts and Crafts Movement*, Trefoil, London, 1983.

Richardson, Tim, *English Gardens in the Twentieth Century: From the Archives of Country Life*, Aurum Press, London, 2005.

Ridley, Jane, *The Architect and His Wife: A Life of Edwin Lutyens*, Chatto & Windus, London, 2001.

Robinson, William, *The English Flower Garden*, John Murray, London, 1883.

—, *Garden Design and Architects' Gardens*, John Murray, London, 1892.

—, *Gravetye Manor, or Twenty Years' Work around an Old Manor House*, John Murray, London, 1911.

—, *Home Landscapes*, John Murray, London, 1920.

—, *The Wild Garden*, John Murray, London, 1870.

Sedding, John D., *Garden-Craft Old and New*, John Lane, London, 1890.

Stamp, Gavin, *Edwin Lutyens Country Houses: From the Archives of Country Life*, Aurum Press, London, 2009.

Stewart-Wilson, Mary, *Queen Mary's Dolls' House*, The Bodley Head, London, 1988.

Strong, Roy, *Country Life, 1897–1997: The English Arcadia*, Boxtree, London, 1996.

Tankard, Judith B., *Gardens of the Arts and Crafts Movement*, Abrams, New York, 2004.

—, and Van Valkenburgh, Michael, *Gertrude Jekyll: A Vision of Garden and Wood*, John Murray, London, 1989.

—, and Wood, Martin, *Gertrude Jekyll at Munstead Wood*, Sutton, Stroud, 1996.

Tipping, H. Avray, *English Gardens*, Country Life, London, 1925.

—, *The Garden of To-Day*, Martin Hopkinson, London, 1933.

Tooley, Michael, and Arnander, Primrose, *Gertrude Jekyll: Essays in the Life of a Working Amateur*, Michaelmas Books, Witton-le-Wear, 1995.

—, and Tooley, Rosanna, *The Gardens of Gertrude Jekyll in Northern England*, Michaelmas Books, Witton-le-Wear, 1982.

Triggs, Harry Inigo, *The Art of Garden Design in Italy*, Longmans, Green & Co., London, 1906.

—, *Formal Gardens in England and Scotland*, B. T. Batsford, London, 1902.

—, *Garden Craft in Europe*, B. T. Batsford, London, 1913.

Wallinger, Rosamund, *Gertrude Jekyll's Lost Garden: The Restoration of an Edwardian Masterpiece*, Garden Art Press, Woodbridge, 2000.

Watts, Annabel, *Helen Allingham's Cottage Homes Revisited*, Unwin Brothers, Old Woking, 1994.

Waymark, Janet, *Thomas Mawson: Life, Gardens and Landscapes*, Frances Lincoln, London, 2009.

Weaver, Lawrence, *The House and Its Equipment*, Country Life, London, 1912.

—, *Houses and Gardens by E. L. Lutyens*, Country Life, London, 1913.

—, ed., *Small Country Houses of To-Day*, Country Life, London, 1910.

—, ed., *Small Country Houses of To-Day*, vol. 2, Country Life, London, 1919.

—, ed., *Small Country Houses: Their Repair and Enlargement*, Country Life, London, 1914.

Whalley, Robin, *The Great Edwardian Gardens of Harold Peto: From the Archives of Country Life*, Aurum Press, London, 2007.

Willmott, Ellen, *Warley Garden*, Bernard Quaritch, London, 1909.

Wilkinson, Rosaleen, *Townhill Park: The Life and Times of a Gertrude Jekyll Garden*, privately printed, 2004.

Wood, Martin, *The Unknown Gertrude Jekyll*, Frances Lincoln, London, 2006.

ARTICLES

Anon., 'Goddards, Abinger Common, Surrey', *Country Life*, 30 January 1904, 162–71.

Aslet, Clive, 'Le Bois des Moutiers, Normandy', *Country Life*, 21 May 1981, 1418–21; 28 May 1981, 1494–97 .

Baskervyle-Glegg, Diana, 'Bulbs Shine Brightly in Broadway', *Country Life*, 29 January 1998, 40–43.

—, 'Designs for a Garden: Formal Informality', *Country Life*, 26 October 1995, 58–61.

[Cook, E. T.?], 'A House and a Garden [Deanery Garden]', *Country Life*, 9 May 1903, 602–11.

Cooper, Nicholas, 'Barrington Court, Somerset', *Country Life*, 24 May 2007, 146–51.

Cram, Robert Nathan, 'Great Tangley Manor: A Homestead That Dates from the Days of William the Conqueror', *House Beautiful*, April 1926, 457–59.

Cresswell-Turner, Sebastian, 'The Making of Lutyens: Le Bois des Moutiers, Normandy', *Country Life*, 25 March 2009, 46–53.

[Graham, Peter Anderson], 'Lindisfarne Castle, Northumberland', *Country Life*, 7 June 1913, 830–42.

'Great Tangley Manor', *Country Life*, 30 July 1898, 109–11; 6 August 1898, 144–47.

Gunn, Fenja, 'Jekyll's Country Life Style', *Country Life*, 26 August 1993, 46–49.

—, 'Where White Is Right', *Country Life*, 8 December 1994, 38–41.

Haslam, Richard, 'Vann, Surrey', *Country Life*, 26 June 1986, 1816–20.

Hellyer, A. G. L., 'The Seven Gardens of Folly Farm', *Country Life*, 6 July 1961, 6–8.

Hill, Oliver, 'An Architect's Debt to "Country Life"', *Country Life*, 12 January 1967, 70–72.

—, 'The Genius of Edwin Lutyens', *Country Life*, 27 March 1969, 710–12.

Hussey, Christopher, 'Folly Farm, Near Reading', *Country Life*, 28 January 1922, 112–19; 4 February 1922, 146–53.

—, 'Gledstone Hall, West Riding, Yorkshire', *Country Life*, 13 April 1935, 374–79; 20 April 1935, 400–05.

—, 'Hestercombe, Somerset', *Country Life*, 16 April 1927, 598–605; 23 April 1927, 638–45.

—, 'Lambay Island', *Country Life*, 20 July 1929, 86–94; 27 July 1929, 120–26.

—, 'Maryland, Hurtwood, Surrey', *Country Life*, 24 October 1931, 452–58.

—, 'Marsh Court, Hampshire', *Country Life*, 19 March 1932, 316–22; 26 March 1932, 354–59.

—, 'Owlpen Old Manor, Gloucestershire', *Country Life*, 2 November 1951, 1460–63; 9 November 1951, 1544–47.

—, 'Plumpton Place, Sussex', *Country Life*, 20 May, 1933, 522–33.

—, 'A Week-end Cottage, Valewood Farm, Sussex', *Country Life*, 21 September 1935, 298–303.

Huxley, Anthony, 'A Lesson in Labour-Saving: The Gardens at Vann, Hambledon, Surrey', *Country Life*, 27 May 1976, 1394–95.

Jekyll, Gertrude, 'Colour in the Flower Garden', in William Robinson, *The English Flower Garden: Style, Position, and Arrangement* (John Murray, London, 1883).

—, 'The Garden', in A. C. Benson and Lawrence Weaver, eds., *The Book of the Queen's Dolls' House* (Methuen, London, 1924).

—, 'Garden Furniture', *Country Life*, 23 May 1925, CXXXVII–CXL.

—, 'Garden Ornament', *Country Life*, 20 February 1926, LXXXV–LXXXVI.

—, 'Historical Notes on Garden Ornament', *Country Life*, 4 and 11 November 1911, 662–64, 701–02 .

—, 'In the Garden: Mr. Thackeray Turner's Garden at Westbrook, Surrey', *Country Life*, 24 July 1915, 119–21.

—, 'In the Garden: Warley Gardens in Spring and Summer', *Country Life*, 12 November 1910, 689–91.

—, 'Millmead, Bramley, Surrey', *The Garden*, 22 March 1919, 130–31.

—, 'On Garden Design Generally', in Lawrence Weaver, ed., *The House and Its Equipment* (Country Life, London, 1912).

—, 'Orchards, Surrey', *Country Life*, 31 August 1901, 272–79.

—, 'Preface', in E. T. Cook, *Gardening for Beginners: A Handbook to the Garden* (Country Life, London, 1901).

—, 'St. Catherine's Court, Somersetshire', *Country Life*, 24 November and 1 December 1906, 738–47, 774–78.

Lemmon, Ken, 'Lutyens with Jekyll Survivals: Gardens of Gledstone Hall, North Yorkshire', *Country Life*, 31 December 1981, 2292–94 .

Longville, Tim, 'Miss Jekyll's Island Foray [Lindisfarne Castle]', *Country Life*, 9 September 2004, 173–79.

Mako, Marion, 'Painting with Nature in Broadway, Worcestershire', *Garden History*, Vol. 34, No. 1 (2006), 47–63.

Massingham, Betty, 'New Life for a Classical Garden [Hestercombe]', *Country Life*, 23 September 1976, 822–26.

Musson, Jeremy, 'Owlpen Manor, Gloucestershire', *Country Life*, 28 September 2000, 106–10.

—, 'Westbrook, Surrey', *Country Life*, 16 July 1998, 50–53.

Newman, Carol, 'Gardens for Cocktail Time', *Country Life*, 14 November 1996, 50–53.

Phillipps, Evelyn March, 'Marshcourt, Hampshire', *Country Life*, 1 September 1906, 306–16.

Phillips, R. Randal, 'Townhill Park, Near Southampton', *Country Life*, 21 April 1923, 536–41.

—, 'Valewood Farm, Haslemere', *Country Life*, 13 October 1928, 523–25.

—, 'Wood House Copse, Holmbury St. Mary, Abinger', *Country Life*, 16 October 1926, 593–94.

Powers, Alan, 'Charm of the Chameleon', *Country Life*, 1 October 1987, 158–61.

—, 'Coleton Fishacre, Devon', *Country Life*, 25 October 2007, 66–72.

Roper, Lanning, 'A Garden of Vistas: Folly Farm, Sulhamstead', *Country Life*, 15 May 1975, 1230–32.

Sales, John, 'Themes on a Londonderry Air', *Country Life*, 17 May 1990, 180–87.

Schilling, Tony, and Schilling, Victoria, 'Touch of Wild: Gravetye Manor', *Country Life*, 3 April 1997, 88–95.

'T' [H. Avray Tipping?], 'Hestercombe, Somerset', *Country Life*, 10 October 1908, 486–94; 17 October 1908, 522–32.

—, 'Orchards, Surrey', *Country Life*, 11 April 1908, 522–30.

Tankard, Judith B., 'Gardening with Country Life', *Hortus*, Summer 1994.

—, 'Gertrude Jekyll, Photographer', *Country Life*, 4 January 1990, 40–41.

—, 'Miss Jekyll's True Colours', *Country Life*, 15 May 1997, 140–43.

—, 'Moon Scape', *Country Life*, 9 May 1996, 72–73 .

—, 'A Perfect Understanding', *Country Life*, 2 March 1995, 48–49.

—, 'Where Flowers Bloom in the Sands', *Country Life*, 12 March 1998, 82–85.

Taylor, G. C., 'Mount Stewart, County Down', *Country Life*, 12 October 1935, 380–86.

Tipping, H. Avray, 'Millmead, Bramley', *Country Life*, 11 May 1907, 674–77.

—, ?, 'Great Tangley Manor', *Country Life*, 21 January 1905, 90–100.

—, ?, 'Owlpen Manor, Gloucestershire', *Country Life*, 6 October 1906, 486–491.

—, ?, 'Tigbourne Court, Witley, Surrey', *Country Life*, 23 September 1905, 414–22.

Weaver, Lawrence, 'Lambay, Ireland', *Country Life*, 4 May 1912, 650–58.

—, 'Marshcourt, Hampshire', *Country Life*, 19 April 1913, 562–71.

—, 'Westbrook, Godalming', *Country Life*, 20 January 1912, 92–96.

Worsley, Giles, 'Goddards, Surrey', *Country Life*, 28 November 1991, 50–53.

Index